TWENTIETH CENTURY
SEASIDE
ARCHITECTURE

THE CASINO AND PLEASURE BEACH, BLACKPOOL.

TWENTIETH CENTURY
SEASIDE
ARCHITECTURE

Kathryn Ferry

BATSFORD

For Michael and Vanessa, who first took me to the seaside

First published in the United Kingdom in 2025 by
Batsford
43 Great Ormond Street
London
WC1N 3HZ

An imprint of B. T. Batsford Holdings Limited

ISBN 978 1 84994 937 8

A CIP catalogue record for this book is available from the British Library.

10 9 8 7 6 5 4 3 2 1

Reproduction by Rival Colour Ltd, UK
Printed by Toppan Leefung Printing International Ltd, China

This book can be ordered direct from the publisher at www.batsfordbooks.com, or try your local bookshop

MIX
Paper | Supporting
responsible forestry
FSC® C104723
www.fsc.org

Sea Terminal, Douglas, Isle of Man. RT.348

CONTENTS

INTRODUCTION

'… the greatest asset a seaside town has is its character of being a seaside town.'

THE ARCHITECTURAL REVIEW, JANUARY 1938

Britain invented the seaside as a place for pleasure, a managed shoreline distinct from the untamed or working coast. From small 17th-century beginnings, domestic tourism by the sea grew into a highly lucrative industry that has left a rich architectural legacy. In the Georgian era pioneering resorts welcomed upper-class health tourists to their clifftop terraces and assembly rooms. During Queen Victoria's reign the railway democratized access to the beach, along with the piers, winter gardens, aquaria and towers that set the scene for the truly mass appeal of the 20th century.

More recently the fabled 'death' of the British seaside has turned it into a by-word for decline and deprivation, resorts killed off by the inexorable rise of cheap foreign package holidays from the 1960s onwards. Though evidence suggests the picture was far more nuanced, the conventional narrative records a sort of stasis after World War II. Seaside architecture of the 1930s is presented as a peak of modernist optimism that was crushed by years of resort closure during hostilities, the downhill trajectory hastened by lack of investment and vision postwar.

It is undeniable that the British seaside underwent huge changes during the 20th century, but the lifeblood of all resorts was novelty, and there was a lot more happening along seafronts than has generally been acknowledged. Some resorts had a limited lifespan; others were so well established that the existing townscape offered few opportunities to modernize. Whereas development phases were affected by changing fashions and local factors, the best buildings always responded to their location on the coastal fringe by adopting a holiday mood, soaking up some extra salt and vinegar and making nautical playfulness a priority. The importance of much seaside architecture has been fleeting, and it is perhaps this sense of ephemerality that explains the tendency to neglect buildings that actually tell a fascinating story of social change and shifts in leisure practice, between 1920 and the Millennium.

Probably no other architectural genre is so well documented through the pictorial format of postcards. Many millions were sold and posted every year, with numerous publishers recording the same buildings and stretches of seafront from different angles at different times. The illustrations in this book are avowedly nostalgic, not just because of the architecture but because of the fashions, the cars, even the heightened colour saturation. In these pieces of printed cardboard, holidaymakers could transmit multiple messages to family and friends back home, not just about the weather but about their tastes and aspirations. When someone chose a picture of a newly built attraction they were proclaiming their choice of destination as modern and worthy of envy. This was pertinent between the wars as competition between resorts intensified, but it continued to be a significant factor as greetings from Blackpool and Southend tumbled onto doormats alongside postcards from Benidorm and beyond. British seaside resorts fought hard for their share of the visitor market. This is the untold story of seaside architecture in the 20th century.

Previous page Seaside buildings evolved to suit changing fashions. This image shows the 1930s pavilion on Weston-super-Mare's Grand Pier paired with a 1970s entrance.

I

INTERWAR
CLASSICAL

LEAS CLIFF CONCERT HALL AND BEACH, FOLKESTONE.

Previous page This side view of Folkestone's 1927 concert hall suggests the impressive views available from its terraces, which were built out from the cliff. **Below** Curved shelters were a crucial part of Blackpool's North Promenade extension in the early 1920s.

THREE PROMENADES, N.S., BLACKPOOL.

213377

Twentieth-century architecture was shaped by the development of modernism, which arrived in Britain in the 1930s and evolved over ensuing decades. It was not the only choice open to architects, but for those places and projects that sought to stand out, it was the most likely to elicit acclaim. This book, however, begins in the 1920s, *before* modernism, in a transition period that has tended to be overlooked. As this chapter will show, the shift towards a cleaner aesthetic was already underway. Influenced by Edwardian classicism, seafronts took on a new whiteness that consigned the Victorian love of colourful cast iron to the past. Building types that had become seaside staples thanks to the technological and decorative potential of iron were now reimagined in pared-down concrete and faience. Designs for new pavilions, winter gardens, bathing pools, bandstands and shelters all underwent this revision in a bid to present themselves as the products of forward-looking resorts.

On the face of it, political and economic circumstances should have made for a quiet decade at the seaside as post-World War I depression was followed by industrial downturns, the 1926 General Strike and the Wall Street Crash of 1929. Nevertheless, visitors kept coming. In 1923 and 1924 fine weather at Easter and Whitsun encouraged record-breaking crowds to flock to the coast, an increasing number of them arriving by road in charabancs, forerunner of modern coaches. Even in the mining communities of South Wales, which suffered mass unemployment and wrenching poverty, people clung tenaciously to their annual day trip to Barry Island as a release from the cares that otherwise pressed upon them. For those in work, the prospect of paid holidays was slowly becoming a reality, so that by mid-decade around one in six of all wage earners were covered by some form of agreement. Although legislative endorsement of holidays with pay was slow in coming, other government policies were to have a profound impact on resort development.

The Health Resorts and Watering Places Act of 1921 was a seemingly modest bill that ultimately proved to be a major breakthrough for local authorities. It allowed borough and urban district councils to spend the income they received from hiring out deckchairs and wheeled bathing machines, as well as admission charges to any municipally administered attraction, on promoting their resort in guides, railway posters and newspaper adverts. The majority of resorts took advantage of this extension to their powers and, moreover, interpreted the terms of the act as an opportunity to expand provision of municipal amenities on an unprecedented scale. Figures for money spent became a weapon in the publicity arsenal as competition between resorts intensified. Paradoxically, high unemployment in seasonal seaside economies supported this interwar burst of activity because

Two vast promenade shelters
at Barry Island provided
covered space for thousands
of day trippers.

from December 1920 local authorities were able to apply to the newly created Unemployment Grants Committee for help with public-works schemes. Financial assistance had previously been restricted to building roads and houses but over the next two decades direct labour was used to construct everything from boating lakes to bathing pools.

With so much responsibility for tourism infrastructure now devolved to local government, borough engineers, surveyors and architects became pre-eminent. The men (and they were all men) who held these roles had the power to shape and define a wider resort vision yet have rarely been given due credit for their successes. Though they were not part of the metropolitan architectural elite they were all connected through the Institution of Municipal and County Engineers and took great interest in the emerging discipline of town planning. This was particularly relevant for seaside towns that had to juggle the competing demands of visitors and residents within the constraints of a geography that gave them half the potential area for expansion enjoyed by inland towns. While resorts could stretch along the seafront and behind it, there was a limit to how much land they could reclaim from the sea. Along the promenade, however, classical and Beaux-Arts styling, inspired by contemporary French and American examples, gave 1920s seaside buildings a new civic grandeur. It was a grandeur that also aspired to Georgian elegance, looking back a century to the early days of the seaside before mass transport opened up the coast.

One of the most widely used forms was the classical colonnade, an open line of columns typically finished in this period with Tuscan capitals of the simplest type. It was particularly well suited to seaside shelters, which were an important resort amenity because landladies generally locked guests out of their boarding houses between mealtimes, whatever the weather. Blackpool's first classical shelter on Princess Parade dates from 1912 and was part of the sea defences subsequently extended along the North Shore during the early 1920s. The new promenade was really three, as can be seen in the postcard on page 12, with the top-road level then a Middle Walk featuring five curved Tuscan shelters and a lower path by the beach. At the northern end, out of view, the first shelter to be built was the grandest, its paired columns accessed via a monumental entrance

BARRY BEACH.

W1879

Herne Bay's 1925 shelter was
designed to fit in with the clock
tower of 1837.

of four concrete pillars swagged with shells, seaweed and fish, and crowned with giant urns. Similarly impressive entrance pillars can be seen in the postcard of South Shore paddling pool (page 24) designed by the same person, John Charles Robinson, who took up the post of chief architectural assistant under borough surveyor Francis Wood in 1920. Robinson had worked as managing assistant to Sir Banister Fletcher for three years before the war, then volunteered for the Artists Rifles, a London army regiment founded by painters, musicians, actors and architects in 1859. After being demobbed he found a job in His Majesty's Office of Works but it was in Blackpool that his architectural talents found fertile ground. From 1925 the new North Shore shelters took centre stage in railway posters advertising the town.

At Barry Island, the pair of oversized shelters dominating Whitmore Bay (page 15), show how the colonnade form could be expanded to meet local demand. A meteoric rise had seen this South Wales resort become the third most popular day-tripper destination in the country after Blackpool and the recently opened Wembley Empire Stadium. New sea walls were needed and their integrated shelters, designed by borough surveyor

J C Pardoe, would benefit visitors as well as the out-of-work labourers recruited to build them. The first one, opened in April 1924, included six shops and lavatory accommodation. Its flat roof extended the promenade area by a third of an acre, creating space for open-air band concerts and dances.

On the County Durham coast at Seaton Carew colonnaded shelters were also a key component of the promenade works opened by Princess Mary in August 1926. Borough engineer Francis Durkin designed the North and South Shelters to hold up to 1,500 people each, most of them day visitors from the nearby industrial town of Hartlepool. Just like at Barry Island, staircases provided access to their flat reinforced concrete roofs.

Shelters in Kent took a more ornamental approach to the basic classical form. The 1925 postcard of Herne Bay's new shelter (opposite), shows Italianate arches framing the central toilet block with columns at either end. At Ramsgate, architect Sir John James Burnet provided Winterstoke Gardens with a semi-circular 'sun shelter', its convex front edged with pairs of Tuscan columns. Southport's Crescent Shelter of 1931 also

New Shelter and Clock Tower, Herne Bay

East View of New Pavilion, Sandbanks.

The 1928 bathing pavilion at Sandbanks in Dorset
was praised for its 'municipal classicism'.

Inside the curve of
Southport's crescent shelter.

formed part of a seafront landscaping project, located on a
processional route through Princes Park with views inland over
the Marine Lake. In the postcard shown right, visitors sit out of
the sea breeze in one of the glazed arms that curved away from
a pedimented central bay; above their heads, decorative beams
extended the shelter's roofline to suggest the effect of an Italian
loggia on the Lancashire coast.

Tuscan colonnades also provided sheltered space in
buildings designed for other seaside purposes. Bathing pavilions
were basically blocks of changing accommodation that visitors
wishing to swim in the sea were encouraged to use for payment
of a small fee. Undressing on the beach was frowned upon well
into the 1930s but hiring an old-fashioned bathing machine
was not an appealing prospect for young holidaymakers; these
cumbersome vehicles had been invented as horse-drawn changing
rooms back in the mid-18th century. To maintain a useful source
of income, local authorities designed new facilities like the 1928
colonnaded pavilion in the postcard shown opposite at Sandbanks
in Dorset. On two sides of an angled crescent, Poole borough
engineer E J Goodacre offered visitors the option of sea-facing

CRESCENT SHELTER, KINGS GARDENS, SOUTHPORT.

213214. J.V.

beach huts for day, week and seasonal hire, or short-hire cubicles facing the car park. A Beaux-Arts-style copper dome crowned the central walkway through to the sands while a balustraded flat roof carried on Tuscan columns provided an elevated space for deckchairs. Members of the Sandbanks Property Owners' Association feared opening of the bathing pavilion would see their secluded beach become 'like Margate'. The *Swanage Times*, on the other hand, praised the building's municipal classicism for its civilizing influence on this previously uncultivated stretch of coast, enthusiastically reporting that visitor numbers had never been so large.[1]

If Sandbanks didn't ultimately become a populist paradise, Margate's reputation was well deserved. As one of the country's oldest resorts it had grown on the profits made from sea-bathing Londoners since at least the 1750s. In 1922 the council's Entertainments Committee noted how city excursionists still 'seemed to come down with the main object of getting into the water', and determined to build a magnificent new bathing pavilion for their comfort. Around the same time, construction of Margate's new Southern Railway station was underway, itself an exemplar of interwar classicism designed by the young Edwin

Maxwell Fry. Holidaymakers were to be funnelled through the gracious space of his Beaux-Arts booking hall in a straight line towards a T-shaped pier 65m (214ft) long on Marine Sands. Opened in July 1926, the pavilion at its end featured three so-called 'saloons', blocks of male and female changing cubicles separated by a central café above the waves. The steel-framed building in the postcard opposite was covered in rusticated boarding between wood pilasters, which the *East Kent Times and Mail* described as being 'designed after the Tuscan style of architecture, this style being the most suitable for construction in timber'. From this grand platform, up to 320 bathers at a time could descend stairways directly into the sea in an arrangement that Margate Council confidently proclaimed would make them 'the envy of all other resorts'.[2]

In fact, other developments were already taking bathing provision in a different direction. The first salt-water pool designed to outwit the tides opened in Scarborough's South Bay in July 1915. Borough engineer Harry W Smith first proposed it in 1900 as a means of seizing back the initiative from newer competing resorts, but construction as part of a robust sea-

Marine Bathing Pavilion, Margate.

Open Air Bath, and Victoria Pier.

Entrance, the Bath.

OPEN AIR BATH

Open Air Bath.

BLACKPOOL SS C33.

Open Air Bath.

Open Air Bath.

Exterior and interior views of the vast Open Air Baths built opposite Blackpool Pleasure Beach in 1923.

defence scheme only began in April 1914; special dispensation was later given for work to continue after the outbreak of war. Above the pool, changing cubicles were entered through a colonnade and Smith used Italianate details for the subsidiary buildings. Here, then, was the prototype for the lidos that came to be associated with art deco and modernism but which grew out of Edwardian classicism. In 1916, the smart resort of St Anne's in Lancashire opened its newest attraction, 'in the shape of a "Roman" open air swimming bath', designed by Accrington architect Fred Harrison. The *Fleetwood Chronicle* praised it as the work of a most progressive Urban District Council: 'The buildings – the dressing rooms, the café, and the machinery and administration departments – are all of classical and beautiful design, their façades adorned with Ionic pillars and their flat roofs laid out as promenades.'[3] Nearby Blackpool took note and proposed to build two bathing pools the following year. Nothing happened until after the arrival of J C Robinson, under whose influence the first decade of outdoor-pool design reached its apogee. Proclaimed in 1923 as 'A New Colosseum', Blackpool Open Air Baths (opposite) cost the enormous sum of almost £80,000.[4]

Blackpool's D-shaped pool measured 115 × 52m (376 × 172ft) and could hold 7.3 million litres (1.6 million gallons) of filtered sea water. The concourse running around it was over 500m (a third of a mile) long and, when full, the oval amphitheatre could accommodate 8,000 spectators and 1,500 swimmers. Construction began at Christmas 1921 and as the ferro-concrete structure went up it was given a permanent whiteness by the application of faience brick cladding from Shaws of Darwen. Around the exterior, fluted columns broke the two floors of tripartite windows into bays of a punchy, factory-style rhythm. On the eastern elevation the main entrance was impossible to miss, rising up to the tip of a glazed Beaux-Arts dome and accessed through a pair of tall columns more suggestive of a neo-classical bank building. As Allan Brodie and Matthew Whitfield have observed, it was 'as much a civic celebration as a leisure facility'.[5] Directly under the dome was a café that opened onto outdoor terraces with jaunty pergola-style roofs. The postcard on page 25 shows the colonnades that swept around the inner ring in front of the changing cubicles, with spectators looking down from their flat roofs. On the opposite beach-side of the building the main

CHILDREN'S PADDLING POOL, NEW PROMENADE,
S.S. BLACKPOOL.

Even the South Shore paddling pool was given classical
grandeur by Blackpool's borough architect J C Robinson.

Open Air Bath, S. S. Blackpool

Robinson's Open Air Baths were likened to a new Colosseum.

Southport's 1928 Sea Bathing
Lake referenced the design
of Blackpool baths in its
domed entrance.

seating was spread over 11 tiers. In 1937 an account of recent
seaside architecture published in *Official Architect* singled out
Mr Robinson's very fine swimming pool, 'which in its restfulness
to the eye, strained by the surrounding glare, refutes those who
would speak slightingly of the Classic'.[6]

At the end of the 1920s there was still architectural
mileage in the colonnaded style, and Blackpool's South Shore
baths attracted 4 million people during its first six years of
operation. Southport had invested in a Sea Bathing Lake as early
as 1914, when borough engineer Alfred Ernest Jackson was just
two years into his job of reshaping the resort's seafront. By 1926
it was thought to lack sophistication, so a new site was chosen in
Princes Park, part of a huge space reclaimed by tipping refuse onto
low-lying estuarine land. Jackson's second pool design required
the council to borrow £60,000, which was offset by the creation
of 300 jobs. Opened in 1928, the new Sea Bathing Lake (opposite)
and its enclosure were oval, the amphitheatre style clearly inspired
by Blackpool and making more than passing reference to its rival
in the imposing café building with glazed dome. Overall, however,
the architectural effect was less formal. The Tuscan colonnade

ORCHESTRAL PIAZZA & BATHING POOL, SKEGNESS.

R · H · JENKINS, *engineer* JOHN WILLS & SONS, *architects*.

Skegness was so proud of its
joint music and swimming venue
that postcards were produced
of the architect's drawing.

that framed the view outside the café held up a pergola roof and along the 70m (230ft) verandah enclosing the western side of the pool, white wooden spars projected under a gentle pitch of green tiles. Spectators on the tiered seating below could look out over the pool's open east side towards the wider parkland, making Jackson's design a highly appropriate one for a resort that promoted itself as a garden city by the sea.

On the east coast, Skegness was still a relative newcomer among resorts. Before investing in its own bathing pool, the council sent a deputation, including borough surveyor Rowland Henry Jenkins, to report on recent improvements at Blackpool, Lytham St Anne's, Southport, Morecambe and New Brighton. The £40,000 scheme they sanctioned in 1924 aimed to do something none of those places had, by uniting the popularity of bathing with musical entertainments. The design produced by Jenkins, with Skegness and Derby architects John Wills & Sons, was reproduced as a postcard. Its central feature was a shared bandstand between the open-air pool and grandly titled Orchestral Piazza (opposite). Classical colonnades imposed a uniformity across the different site elements and on the promenade the complex

was fronted by a Grand Pavilion housing a café; this would later become the Embassy Ballroom. As construction began in May 1927 the *Boston Guardian* anticipated that future visitors would 'be able to spend the whole of the day at a minimum of expense and gain a maximum of enjoyment and invigorating exercise'.[7] The bathing pool opened a year later, attracting over 300,000 admissions during its first season. As for the bandstand, the domed rotunda design was as much a mark of modernity as the concept it embodied. Victorian 'birdcage' bandstands in cast iron were familiar features of parks throughout the land but people on holiday had more time to enjoy outdoor concerts and competitive pressure at coastal resorts resulted in a design variation specific to the seaside.

The first classical bandstands appeared before World War I. Their precursors survive in the two rotunda shelters of J B Wall's curved colonnade at Bexhill-on-Sea in East Sussex, marking the coronation of George V in 1911 and explicitly alluding to the architecture of previous Georgian reigns. In 1912 a circular domed bandstand was installed in the Lord Street Municipal Gardens at Southport. This was followed by the 11m (37ft) high

The Band Promenade, Hastings

The domed roof of Hastings' 1916 pier bandstand
was replicated in the timber shelters on either side.

Bandstand and Lake, Stanley Park, Blackpool.

A crowd of holidaymakers gathers around the newly
built bandstand in Blackpool's Stanley Park.

bandstand in the postcard on page 30, erected on the promenade extension to Hastings Pier in 1916. The most obvious prototype was the 18th-century garden temple, a folly or focal point in aristocratic pleasure grounds, exemplified by William Chambers' 1763 design for the Temple of Aeolus at Kew Gardens. Twentieth-century interpretations used concrete instead of stone columns but the garden context was an important point of parallel. Seaside resorts everywhere invested in landscaping to create pleasure grounds for the masses. Hastings had been losing its appeal since the turn of the century, so the new pier bandstand was part of a wider scheme to lay out the nine acres of council-owned White Rock Gardens with flower beds, rockeries, two bowling greens, croquet lawns and tennis courts. More temple-like bandstands followed after the war, notably at St Lawrence Gardens, Ramsgate, (opposite), built in 1926, the same year as one at Vale Park, New Brighton. Edward Prentice Mawson used the form at Blackpool's Stanley Park in 1929 and the restored Blyth seafront example of 1934 is still in occasional use.

Through the 1930s the domes of bandstands evolved a shallower profile. The most famous survivor is the 1935 Central Bandstand at Eastbourne (page 34), designed in the office of borough surveyor Major Leslie Roseveare. This took the form of a band 'enclosure' where the performance space was part of a larger building with colonnaded shelters around the edge of an open-air auditorium. Like the Victorian bandstand it replaced, the Eastbourne enclosure was built on the beach, supported on nine 6m (20ft)-long iron pillars sunk into the bedrock beneath the sand. It could seat 3,000 people, a third of them under cover, and became a much-loved landmark thanks to its strikingly squat double-dome tiled in azure blue. The whole building is a fine display of the 'ceramic marble' made by Carter & Co. of Poole, with blue and green tiles offsetting the stone colour of the colonnades. Though there is a hint of art deco in its geometric frieze, the Central Bandstand is better understood as belonging to the well-established interwar classicism that also inspired the lost 1937 marina band enclosure at Great Yarmouth and the surviving 1939 bandstand at Wellington Crescent Gardens on Ramsgate's east cliff.

Part of the reason these more conservative designs continued to be built, even as architectural currents shifted in the 1930s, has to do with the complex requirement for seaside

ST. LAWRENCE CLIFF BANDSTAND, RAMSGATE.

Eastbourne's tiled band enclosure in the
1950s. It is still a popular concert venue.

PIER ENTRANCE AND BANDSTAND, WORTHING.

Worthing's Pier Pavilion and Bandstand were
both designed by Adshead and Ramsey.

THE PIER PAVILION, WORTHING.

H.9538.

This late 1930s view of Worthing Pier illustrates the contrast between the 1920s neo-Georgian pavilion and the moderne structures built along its length in 1935.

resorts to appear simultaneously progressive *and* moderate, to cater for the different classes of staying visitors and day trippers. Reviewing the new band enclosure and pier pavilion at Worthing in 1926, the *Architects' Journal* concluded that Messrs Adshead and Ramsey had created 'a most remarkable piece of psychology … [The two buildings] hold the balance between the retired colonel and the happy tripper with astounding precision.'[8] Both structures can be seen in the postcard on page 35, the band enclosure for summer excursionists raised on a platform over the beach with arcs of glazed screens either side of its stage terminating in Beaux-Arts kiosks on the promenade. The pier pavilion (opposite) was intended to consolidate Worthing's position as one of England's leading winter resorts, famous for its year-round sunshine record. Though it quickly came to seem old-fashioned, when compared with new pier buildings added in the 1930s, Stanley Davenport Adshead assured dignitaries gathered for the opening ceremony that Worthing had got the 'last word in pavilions'. It was, he said, unbeaten by anywhere he had seen in the cultural capitals of New York, Paris, Rome or Vienna.[9] Adshead's professional credentials certainly lent weight to his claims. A friend and former colleague of

Charles Reilly, at the influential Liverpool School of Architecture, and himself a professor at London University since 1914, Adshead had been introduced to the American classicism of McKim, Mead and White by his architectural partner Stanley Churchill Ramsey, and enjoyed a national reputation in the nascent field of town planning. His first solo commission was the 1904 Royal Victoria Pavilion at Ramsgate, a less refined version of what he produced for Worthing, where he allowed the rounded roof to steal the show. Built side-on to the pier to spread its weight better, the walls of Worthing's steel-framed concert hall were kept submissively low, with the entrance approach carefully planned to draw the eye from side kiosks, along curved service wings, towards the raised foyer. Adshead described the architectural style as 'an essay in modern Classic'. Inside, the roof trusses were left visible with blue and gold paint used to produce a 'bright and sunny effect'.[10] As seen in the postcard on page 38, the walls were covered in trelliswork and large, tasselled light fixtures added a flavour of art deco chinoiserie, so that the interior might be seen as a foreshadowing of the neo-Georgian trend Osbert Lancaster later nicknamed 'Vogue Regency'.[11] Other seaside pavilions, at Weston-super-Mare and Folkestone, also favoured royal

INTERIOR PIER PAVILION, WORTHING. 18

Inside Worthing Pier Pavilion the steel frame was left exposed with painted trelliswork added to suggest an 18th-century orangery or winter garden.

THE BEACH BALLROOM, ABERDEEN

The classical entrance front of Aberdeen's 1926 Beach Ballroom.

The domed pavilion at Weston-super-Mare shielded extensive formal gardens from the breezy seafront beyond.

blue and gold interiors, with similar provision of a promenade ring around the hall so the space could be used for dancing.

The importation from America of first ragtime, then jazz, spurred a succession of crazes that made a well-sprung dance floor a must for resorts. In 1926 Aberdeen added a Beach Ballroom (page 39), designed by Roberts and Hume of Bathgate, to its seaside amenities. The main space was topped by a highly visible pitched roof of red pantiles that contrasted with the buff faience of the single-storey entrance front. Dancers walked through the Ionic columns of the main doorway into a hall that was originally open to the full height of its octagonal dome. Much of the classical decorative scheme survives, although it is now under a false ceiling. Thankfully the elliptical dome at Weston-super-Mare's Winter Gardens Pavilion remains intact. This building was the centrepiece of the council's new Marine Parade, laid out from 1922 on what had been a patch of open ground. Landscape architect and town planner Edward Mawson assisted the borough surveyor Harold Brown on a £35,000 scheme that included extensive formal gardens and a 33m (108ft) lily pond framed by colonnaded walks, as seen in the postcard opposite. Like at Worthing, the council

PAVILION AND WINTER GARDENS, WESTON-SUPER-MARE.

Grand Pavilion, (showing Entrance to Gardens) Porthcawl. 878

Porthcawl's 1932 Grand
Pavilion combined classical
colonnades with an art
deco-style clock tower.

hoped to attract 'off-season' business but the need to maintain sea views of existing properties required the pavilion's ballroom floor to be sunk 1.4m (4ft 6in) below ground level. A souvenir brochure produced for the 1927 opening described the main hall as a 'spectacle of thrilling wonderment' for the way its graceful curves were left in the simplicity of their unadorned state.[12] Along the façade, open Tuscan colonnades (filled in during the 1990s) allowed people to stroll between town and beach through the gardens. Porthcawl's 1932 Grand Pavilion (opposite) also featured open loggia-style shelters and arches that led to a rear garden. This was probably more than coincidence because paddle-steamer services operating across the Bristol Channel placed resorts on the Somerset and South Wales coasts in direct competition for visitors from the Welsh industrial heartlands. The £25,000 Grand Pavilion was designed by E J E Moore, with L G Mouchel and Partners as consultants for its ferro-concrete dome. That this building belongs to a transition period can be seen in the art deco angles of the striking clocktower above its otherwise classical entrance.

Design choices were informed by a desire to attract new visitors but there was also a real fear of losing the wealthy patrons of the past to Continental destinations, particularly where there was no other industry to fall back on. At the opening of the Leas Cliff Hall in July 1927, Folkestone's mayor bluntly stated that 'we are entirely a first-class health resort, absolutely dependent upon our residential population and the visitors who come here for health and pleasure'. The council was therefore prepared to invest £80,000 in surmounting the constructional challenges of building an exclusive new venue into the cliff face. Local architect John Love Seaton Dahl had to enlarge an existing shelter hall to provide the maximum number of open-air terraces and balconies at the same time as preserving the very view that people came to enjoy. Dahl designed his ferro-concrete building on piers that ran down into deep foundations to support six heavy box girders spanning the 16.5m (54ft) width of the flat promenade roof. The postcard on page 11 shows the upper levels faced in cream terracotta, with Corinthian columns across the front of the main concert hall and colonnaded promenades at either end. The cantilevered balcony used to create extra space is clearly seen in the postcard on page 45, below which the aesthetic was more functional.

LEAS CLIFF HALL AND BEACH, FOLKESTONE.

Local architect John Love Seaton Dahl had to deal
with a challenging clifftop site at Folkestone.

Classical detailing on the upper floors of Leas Cliff Hall gave
way to simpler glazed elevations on the lower levels.

The new Scarborough Spa ballroom before it was connected to the promenade bandstand.

At long-established Scarborough and Brighton, the lack of vacant sites meant that 1920s updates took the form of alterations to existing buildings. Scarborough's famous Spa was still in private hands when, in 1925, its company directors invested £30,000 in a ballroom and café extension at the southern end (opposite). Its tall windows, separated by white Tuscan pilasters, created a clear contrast with the stone of the Victorian pavilion and were later extended to enclose the bandstand on the promenade. Brighton's seafront aquarium was equally important to *its* history and as much in need of a facelift. Built by Eugenius Birch, designer of the town's West Pier, it opened in 1872 as Britain's first public aquarium. Fifty years later it was well past its peak, with a tatty jumble of temporary buildings on its rooftop terraces. Despite this, public outcry at proposals to replace it with a bus garage in 1922 made clear that total demolition was not an option and the council stepped in to buy it for a fraction of its original cost. Borough engineer David Edwards came up with a plan that maintained the principal corridor of fish tanks but cleared away the Victorian east end to make way for a concert and dance hall, refreshment spaces,

rifle range and shops. In April 1928 the London *Daily News* reported that hundreds of people had watched workmen take their sledgehammers to the building: 'Old Brighton was being shattered to make way for the modern and better Brighton.'[14] By June the following year the aquarium had been transformed (page 48): gleaming white balustrades marked the site boundaries, enclosing the light wells above the renovated tanks and linking the decongested roof terraces. The spiky Gothic clock over the entrance was gone, replaced by imposing bronze gates flanked by kiosks with pyramid roofs.

A different variation on the classical theme was adopted for Bournemouth's neo-Georgian pavilion. In 1923 nearly a hundred entries were submitted in a prestigious architectural competition judged by Sir Edwin Cooper. With a very generous budget of £160,000, the pavilion was intended as a monument to Bournemouth's 70-year rise from open heathland to one of the wealthiest resorts in the country. G Wyville Home and Shirley Knight won the commission, though by the time their building opened in 1929 final costs had risen to a contentious £250,000. On a steeply sloping site, the red-brick and stone building was

SPA BANDSTAND AND BALLROOM, SCARBOROUGH

THE AQUARIUM, BRIGHTON.

211487

The 1929 rebuild of Brighton Aquarium brought
a classical clarity to this Victorian landmark.

GARDENS AND PAVILION (ENTRANCE) BOURNEMOUTH.

Bournemouth Pavilion originally had low flanking kiosks
either side of its concert hall entrance.

THE PIER APPROACH, BOURNEMOUTH

Built in red brick and stone like the Pavilion, Bournemouth's Pier Approach Baths opened in 1937 and its new pier entrance in 1939. Both have long since been replaced.

planned in two halves, with the large concert hall accessed from Westover Road; below it, a ballroom, supper room and restaurant faced the seafront. As can be seen in the postcard on page 49, the pantiled pyramid roof of the upper section was originally echoed by two low pavilions either side of the main entrance. Round arched openings and wide classical pilasters under a deep stone cornice all spoke to a stripped classicism that was carried through into the interior, where Greek, Egyptian and Regency influences freely mixed. While the pseudo-Adam theatre decoration of festoons and laurel wreaths is quietly conservative, the mirrored restaurant interiors suggested a brasher new taste, the pavilion's overall character seeking to blend Bournemouth's reputation for refined elegance with its growing mass appeal. In 1937 the indoor Pier Approach Baths were commissioned in matching materials from architect and pool specialist Kenneth Cross. Borough architect F P Dolamore then employed the same red brick and stone to update the pier entrance in 1939 (opposite), completing an unusual set-piece of neo-Georgian resort branding. These structures were the counterpoint to a bolder vision of modernity that will be discussed in the next chapter.

The restrained Italianate of
Hastings White Rock Pavilion
won praise for its suitability for
a seaside setting.

All were proof of a gradual move towards a simplified
aesthetic, with greater clarity of form and reduced ornament, even
though the basic vocabulary remained rooted in past styles. At
Hastings, the 1927 White Rock Pavilion (opposite) won plaudits for
its architectural restraint. The concert hall-cum-cinema-cum-dance
hall replaced the town's Victorian hospital in a clear sign of altered
visitor priorities away from health to enjoyment. Architects Charles
Cowles Voysey and Hugh T Morgan worked in a roughly Italianate
mode, with pyramid-topped roofs to the end wings abutting the
pavilion's bow front. Writing in the *Architects' Journal*, M L Anderson
considered the creamy stuccoed exterior, with its red pantiles and
coloured terracotta plaques, appropriately cheerful and praised the
lack of 'swags and panels which one is accustomed to see in such
buildings at seaside towns'. For a multi-purpose, multi-class venue,
'the wisdom of avoiding all but the freest and simplest of forms is
unquestionable'.[15] Muted tones were used throughout the interior,
with colour supplied by large silk lampshades. This was not yet the
seaside modernism of the 1930s but, as with the extraordinarily
bare dome of Weston-super-Mare's Winter Gardens Pavilion, it
deserves to be seen as advancing in that direction.

White Rock Music Pavilion, Hastings.

M. 259.

2

DECO, MODERN, MODERNE

THE DE LA WAF

ON. BEXHILL-ON-SEA

9049

Previous page A tinted postcard of the De La Warr Pavilion produced soon after its opening in 1935. **Below** An aerial view shows how the 1935 De La Warr Pavilion contrasted with the existing Victorian and Edwardian seafront.

6702   DE LA WARR PAVILION AND COLONNADE, BEXHILL ON SEA.

I n December 1935 the De La Warr Pavilion (opposite) opened at Bexhill-on-Sea in East Sussex. Designed by Erich Mendelsohn and Serge Chermayeff, it brought International Modernism to the British seaside in no uncertain terms. The impetus came from the town's mayor, the Earl De La Warr, whose family had overseen the development of Victorian and Edwardian Bexhill on the edge of their vast estates but whose own socialist politics led to his insistence on good modern design for all. The terms of the 1933 architectural competition specifically discouraged heavy stonework, calling for a light and attractive building. In architectural circles the De La Warr Pavilion was widely perceived as a new start. Mendelsohn was already renowned as one of Germany's leading modernists and, working with the Austrian engineer Felix Samuely, who like him had fled Hitler in 1933, he proposed to build Britain's first welded steel structure. This would be cheaper, quicker to construct and allow for thinner, more streamlined walls and floors. Over the course of just 11 months, a sophisticated lesson in elegant simplicity rose on Bexhill seafront. To the west a plain concrete box housed the multi-purpose entertainments hall while to the east a lower block used steel, glass and glazed tiles to give the restaurant and café uninterrupted sea views. An airy entrance hall linked the two spaces, articulated at front and back by stunning spiral staircases cocooned in glass.

Many of the De La Warr Pavilion's defining features subsequently recurred in buildings elsewhere around the coast. This was not merely copying but an acknowledgement that the forms themselves were exceptionally well suited to the new seaside context. In August 1930 *The Graphic* magazine proclaimed a 'New Bronze Age' as members of the fashionable set flocked to lie in the French Riviera sunshine.[16] Cultivating a suntan caught on as the latest health craze and flat roofs, which had been built in the 1920s for promenading, now became central to the seaside aesthetic as decks for sunbathing. Full-height glazing aided exposure to health-giving UV rays and, in curved stair towers, engineering advances allowed for the ultimate expression of a long-established seaside device, extending the Georgian bow window beyond the wall plane to maximize the sea view. The previous chapter showed how white concrete had already altered the seafront but now the pared-down ornament of the 1920s was removed altogether under the influence of Swiss modernist Le Corbusier and German architect and Bauhaus founder Walter Gropius. At its best the new seaside architecture delivered the clarity of modernism's mantra that form should follow function, that a building's design should begin with its purpose and work from the inside out. But there was another coastal relevance too. Cantilevered curves and decks of sun-trap balconies also referenced the era's most luxurious form of transport, the ocean

One of the entrances to Hastings' pioneering underground car park.

liner, and the elite fashion for cruising. At the British seaside ordinary people boarded buildings instead of boats and looked out across the horizon in a fantasy of 'liners on land'.

The intersection of these trends with what is now known as art deco gave rise to the most prolific of 1930s seaside styles, dubbed by contemporaries as moderne or modernistic. Whereas true modernism was about evolving beyond attached decoration, art deco was based on an ornament of geometric shapes and stylized natural forms that drew on sources as varied as ancient Egypt and American jazz. Named after the hugely influential 1925 Exposition Internationale des Arts Décoratifs et Industriels Modernes in Paris, art deco helped give seaside architecture its all-important mirage of escape from everyday life.

The 1930s was a boom period for seaside resorts. Despite continued depression in traditional manufacturing industries, middle-class living standards were on the rise and political impetus towards holidays with pay finally saw legislation passed in 1938. Most holidaymakers still travelled by train but motor coaches and charabancs increased their market share and generated new building types. With its stocky deco clock tower and streamlined wings, Seaton Carew's 1938 seafront bus station, by borough engineer Francis Durkin, is now the best survivor of its kind. An even bigger impact came from the surging number of private motor cars. As summer traffic jams became part of the holiday experience it was no coincidence that Britain's first municipal underground and multi-storey car parks were built at the seaside, at Hastings (1931, opposite) and Blackpool (1939) respectively. Massive shifts in society and infrastructure requirements made designing for the new leisure environment a challenge with which the architectural press regularly sought to grapple. In July 1936 *The Architectural Review* published drawings by Mendelsohn and Chermayeff that showed a wholesale rethinking of what a seafront could be. Their proposals would have put the De La Warr Pavilion at the centre of a development including a hotel and furnished flat block, a cinema with shops along its ground floor, and an open-air bathing pool with dressing boxes and sun decks that was to terminate in a slender pier, connecting the buildings directly with the sea. These were the facilities of the era and though they never materialized at Bexhill, other resorts did gain similar new structures in a period marked by its optimistic spirit of change and renewal.

THE NEW PARADE. LOOKING EAST HASTINGS

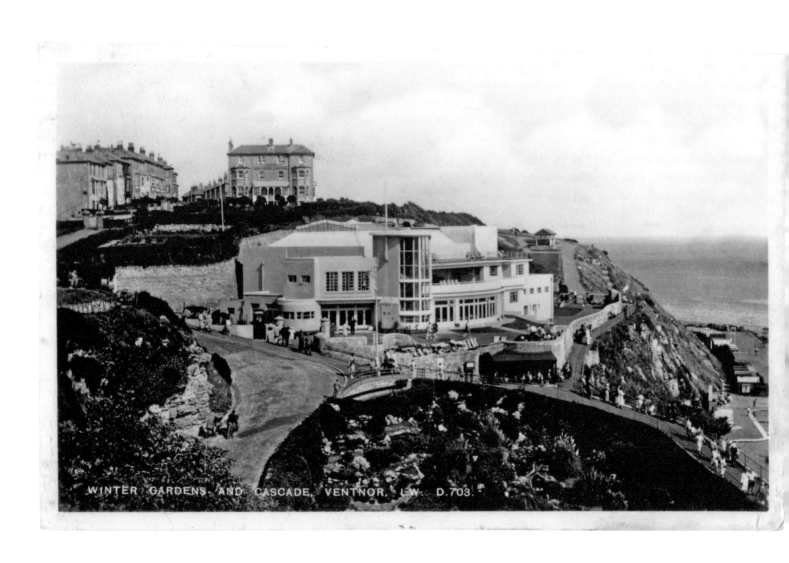

WINTER GARDENS AND CASCADE, VENTNOR, I.W. D.703

Ventnor Winter Gardens has a glazed stair tower inspired by the De La Warr Pavilion.

When the Ventnor Winter Gardens (opposite) opened in August 1936 it was the Isle of Wight's most modern structure, the steel and concrete venue replacing a converted Victorian parsonage. A glazed stair tower rises on the west side and if architect A Douglas Clare did not manage the panache of Bexhill his source of inspiration was nonetheless clear. Scotland's answer to the De La Warr Pavilion was more assured, the 1938 Rothesay Pavilion by James Carrick. Postcard views of the building are extremely rare, but to the scores of Glaswegians arriving by steamer it must have presented a fantastic sight with its asymmetrical design of a round, cantilevered café extending out from the flat-roofed auditorium block. In deference to the weather conditions, Carrick specified a buff-coloured synthetic stone ashlar to clad the concrete walls, while the upper sun deck was coated with Lavacrete for quick drying after rain. Long-planned restoration work to secure the building's future finally got underway in 2023. Carrick's other seaside pavilion, the Cragburn at Gourock in Inverclyde, is now lost. Completed in 1936, the budget was £11,000 compared to £50,000 at Rothesay, which determined a far simpler three-storey block in cement-stucco-clad brickwork with black cornicing. Its rectangular mass was given vertical accents in the six tall windows that broke up the long Clyde-facing frontage. As can be seen in the postcard on page 62, the first-floor sun deck was sensitively designed to echo the window levels of surrounding houses so the pavilion managed to both stand out from, and fit in with, its neighbours.

Few other pavilions and dance halls have been studied by historians because they fall short of the high standards set at Bexhill. Postcard writers rarely commented on architecture yet the words pencilled on the back of the view of Fleetwood's 1935 Marine Hall (page 63) suggest a need to balance the views of critics with those of the visiting public; the sender informed Mr and Mrs Dixon that this was '… a new and modern hall and adds to the attractions of Fleetwood'. Though the domed concrete structure by borough engineer William Melville certainly could not be called pioneering, in its local context the plain cream Portland cement exterior, with green faience string courses and open sun colonnades, *was* visibly novel. And the grounds for claiming modernity went beyond the architectural; hidden lighting that could produce multiple different-coloured effects and bespoke tubular steel chairs were

ASHTON & PAVILION, GOUROCK, FROM THE WATER.   A.3838.

The simple white massing of James Carrick's Cragburn
Pavilion stood out along the Gourock waterfront.

THE MARINE HALL, FLEETWOOD.

Though Fleetwood's Marine Hall paired angular façades with
a Beaux-Arts dome, visitors perceived it as modern.

also touted as innovations. At Bridlington in Yorkshire, the Spa Royal Hall is another surviving 1930s venue featuring a dome and art deco plaster decorations in its ballroom. The hall, which had only opened in 1926, burned down in January 1932. A mammoth rebuilding effort saw it ready for the summer season just 52 days later with a taller, simplified façade and increased glazing. The postcard opposite shows the interior, with angular deco light fixtures complementing the sunburst patterns framing the central dome. At Aberystwyth the 1934 King's Hall, built by L G Mouchel and Partners, formed the corner building of a Victorian terrace, where it was made to stand out by its eye-catching whiteness and a central campanile-style clock tower that played with Italian references and art deco massing on the Welsh coast.

Pleasure piers remained key entertainment venues. Fundamentally Victorian structures, often enlarged with Edwardian entertainment pavilions, they were ripe for the ire of interwar critics who condemned their 'iron bedstead design'.[17] More than one hundred piers had been built to act as promenade extensions and landing stages for paddle steamers. Still functionally important and popular with holidaymakers, they were also highly prone to

disaster. The Grand Pier at Weston-super-Mare lost its pavilion to flames in 1930; Lee-on-the-Solent pier and the Floral Hall on Great Yarmouth's Britannia Pier burned down in 1932. Then in 1933 seven separate pier fires occurred at Bridlington, Worthing, Margate, Morecambe, Southport and twice at Colwyn Bay.

Rebuilding offered the opportunity to modernize. At Colwyn Bay Stanley Adshead was appointed consultant architect working with borough surveyor W J Dunning, on a new fire-proof pier pavilion. Opened in May 1934, it incorporated a theatre, ballroom, café and bar within a light steel structure clad in asbestos. On the entrance front, two cone-capped lanterns paid homage to the turreted pavilion that had burned down, with an original art-deco flavour provided by diagonal louvres and playful finials to give the simple white building its distinctive profile. In the auditorium, murals by Mary Adshead (Stanley's daughter) suggested a marquee supported by ornamental poles and ropes, while café murals by Eric Ravilious featured green and pink seaweed wafting through the ruins of a submerged palace. A review in *The Architect and Building News* praised the building for striking 'exactly the right note in the architecture of pleasure'.[18]

LEE-ON-SOLENT, THE TOWER ENTRANCE TO THE PIER.

80468

A dramatic tower rose above the 1936
entrance to Lee-on-the-Solent Pier.

Worthing Pier's new Sun Pavilion opened in July 1935. Combining a dance hall and circular solarium in a nautical moderne building, corporation architect C H Wallis demonstrated how far architectural tastes had travelled in the decade since construction of Adshead and Ramsey's entrance pavilion. The *Worthing Gazette* reported that 'the general tendency of interior fittings will be to give a ship-board effect … the outside colouring is in sea blues and greens.'[19] Photographs from the opening suggest these colours were used in stripes around the metal-cased plywood cladding, a contrary look to the plain cream modernist vision we're used to seeing today. The 1936 Marine Ballroom on Morecambe Central Pier was also heavily influenced by the liner trend; a central funnel rose from its curved roof and a sun deck above the entrance stood in for the ship's bridge. It was designed by C B Pearson of Lancaster, who was also responsible for the Don Café at the pier entrance. This got its streamlined appearance from taking the basic form of a Georgian bow-fronted house and applying it to four sides of a rectangle, a seaside staple multiplied then modernized with decoration in green and black vitrolite, a type of coloured glass widely used between the wars.

The replacement Lee-on-the-Solent pier in Hampshire was far more ambitious. Cinema architects Yates, Cook and Darbyshire created the 30m (100ft) tower seen in the postcard opposite to give views over the pier from a curved glass observation deck. Slanted wings either side provided a 1,000-seat cinema and a winter garden café suitable for dances, with rhythmic concrete fins across the forecourt elevation painted green. An equally audacious sea-end pavilion was planned but the syndicate of local businessmen backing the resort's modernization went bust within two years and later wartime damage to the pier was never repaired.

At Blackpool, remnants of the 1938 South Pier Pavilion survive under later accretions. Architects R W Hurst and D R Humphrys widened the shore end to create the concert hall in the postcard on page 68. This had an innovative diagrid roof, its intersecting diagonal beams infilled with acoustic board panels and left exposed in a design that complemented the stylized art deco wall decorations by architectural perspectivist Edmund Thring. On the rendered side walls facing the beach, pairs of winged art deco horses rode over geometric waves and a 3.7m (12ft)-high concrete sea horse was cast in situ to surmount the front elevation. These

SOUTH PIER, BLACKPOOL, S.S.

H.383.

Blackpool's South Pier Pavilion featured a giant seahorse
sculpture over the entrance and art deco murals on either side.

PIER FROM THE BRIDGE, CLACTON-ON-SEA.

90B.

Updates to Clacton Pier included the Crystal Casino, left
of the entrance, and the Blue Lagoon dance hall, to the right.

The 1939 Pier Bandstand at Weymouth was demolished
in 1986, though the entrance building survives.

decorative flourishes were accompanied by a bold use of colour: the curved cream payboxes had blue doors with orange window frames and emerald-green canopies. Similar bright tones were employed by Charles Frey Callow, architect to the Hastings Pier Company, in his 1933 updating of the entrance pavilion featuring a hexagonal clock at the centre of a stepped art deco façade. Clacton Pier's (page 69) entrepreneurial owner Ernest Kingsman spent a decade turning the town's old jetty into an amusement hotspot over the sea. By 1934 up to 40,000 people a day were being lured through the turnstiles between the Blue Lagoon dance hall and the Crystal Casino, so-called because it shimmered at night through walls made of glass brick. Though the era of fresh pier building had passed, a new hybrid pier-bandstand opened at Weymouth in 1939, extending 73m (240ft) over the beach. Accessed through a promenade-level loggia, V J Wenning's open auditorium was enclosed either side of the stage by cantilevered shelters that maintained sight lines while protecting at least some of the audience from summer showers. In common with many seaside schemes of the decade, lighting was crucial and Wenning worked with neon specialists Ionlite Ltd, who installed the 762m

(2,500ft) of two-colour neon tubing and 1,200 electric lamps that are lighting up the structure in the postcard shown opposite.

Unlike piers, cinemas proliferated throughout the country, but the intense popularity of movie-going made them a necessity for even the smallest resorts. In 1934 an early Odeon, designed by George E Tonge, opened at Cleveleys in Lancashire. From there the Oscar Deutsch chain spread rapidly, its streamlined house style arriving at Weston-super-Mare and Worthing in 1935, Colwyn Bay, Scarborough, Clacton and Ramsgate in 1936, Morecambe, Rhyl, Lowestoft, Brighton and Bournemouth in 1937, and Blackpool in 1939. An important architectural precursor for these was the Dreamland Cinema at Margate (page 73), part of a scheme to revamp the seafront amusement park begun in 1933 and opened two years later. Owner John Henry Iles borrowed the name from New York's Coney Island but his architects, Julian Leathart and W F Granger, took their inspiration from German expressionism and Berlin cinema design of the 1920s. The brief was a complicated one because the new building had to incorporate an existing ballroom as well as signal access to the rides and sideshows at the rear. Thanks to the vertical brick

The Dreamland Cinema at
Margate, pictured in the 1950s.

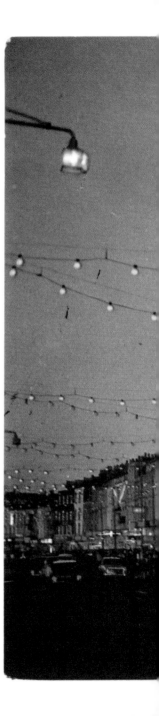

fin that dramatically splits the façade above ground-floor level,
Dreamland's presence, with its name lit up in neon, is unmissable.
Thrill-seeking crowds just had to follow the curve of the entrance
canopy to the fairground.

Seaside amusement parks were a major growth sector
in the 1930s and Billy Butlin was so successful with his coastal
chain that they funded his move into holiday camps. Butlin chose
mid-sized resorts where he could make the biggest impact with
modernistic buildings designed to tempt a middle- and upper-
working-class audience. At Littlehampton in West Sussex his vast
amusement shed had a bold art deco silhouette and red neon
branding. His 1933 Felixstowe park was defined by the stepped
deco corner towers of its café building, still the centrepiece of
Manning's Amusements today. All the showmen who invested
in permanent seaside sites knew the value of architectural
signposting. At New Brighton on the Wirral, George Wilkie's New
Palace amusements used alternating levels of projecting art deco
fins along its 165m (540ft)-long frontage, culminating in the soaring
curved fin seen over the entrance in the postcard on page 74. From
1934 visitors to Southport Pleasureland (page 75) recognized

VICTORIA GARDENS, NEW BRIGHTON.

H.8644

It was hard to miss the entrance fin of Wilkie's
New Palace Amusements at New Brighton.

The Marine Lake from Pleasure Beach, Southport.   ET. 5763

The 1934 art deco entrance tower at Southport
Pleasureland was originally lit up at night.

David Pleydell-Bouverie won critical acclaim for the Rotunda and promenade shelters he built as part of Folkestone's 1938 Foreshore redevelopment.

the entrance there by its 20m (65ft)-high, three-tiered hexagonal tower, likely inspired by a similar design atop the Empire Marketing Board Pavilion at the 1929 North East Coast Exhibition in Newcastle. On the Kent coast, architect David Pleydell-Bouverie made the Rotunda amusement centre (opposite) the showpiece of his Folkestone foreshore redevelopment. This circular structure, intended for sideshows and shooting galleries, was engineered by Felix Samuely using brick infill between the concrete piers holding up its reinforced-concrete saucer dome. Crushed fragments of blue glass rolled into the asphalt roof covering gave an iridescent effect and the interior was lit by circular glass discs flush with the dome's surface.

The most critically acclaimed amusement buildings were designed by Joseph Emberton for Blackpool Pleasure Beach. Emberton's status as a British-born modernist marked him out among the talented emigrés leading the movement and in 1932 his Royal Corinthian Yacht Club at Burnham-on-Crouch, in Essex, was one of a pair of buildings selected to represent England at the International Exhibition of Modern Architecture at New York's Museum of Modern Art. Experience in retail and exhibition

Joseph Emberton transformed Blackpool Pleasure Beach, even overseeing the addition of Cubist animals to the Noah's Ark ride.

design during the 1920s made him the perfect choice for Leonard Thompson, who succeeded his father-in-law as managing director of Blackpool Pleasure Beach in 1933. Over the next six years, Emberton revamped the park, introducing a rational efficiency that successfully dispelled professional snobbery at the same time as using the established fairground sensations of colour, light and movement to satisfy the Blackpool crowds. Most attractions were already in place, so Emberton's job was to give them stylistic coherence, combining streamlined curves with a series of towers that announced each different ride through its form and bright neon signage. The miniature railway station for the Pleasure Beach Express used a giant fin set into a cylindrical tower resting on four circular plates that gave the roof a grill-like effect. For the 1935 Grand National, three curving canopies were cantilevered over the station and dual tracks of the wooden roller coaster, with a cruciform tower rising above their meeting point. The same year saw completion of the world's largest fun palace (opposite), in a new building filled with a bewildering series of shaking, rocking and dropping floors, dark passageways, steep slides and centrifugal drums. Its tower combined cross and fin elements, capped by a

floating concave saucer. The façade was a magnificent expression of its function; letters spelling out the Fun House name rocked endlessly in roundels above a mural of energetic clowns, while a ribcage of extending canopies animated the curved corner of the front elevation. From 1939 the slick, cruise-liner look of Emberton's circular Casino building (page 80) proclaimed the modern pleasure-beach aesthetic towards the promenade, with a slim corkscrew stair that quickly became a Blackpool landmark. There was no gambling in this casino; the name referenced Continental refreshment and entertainment buildings and, in a society still stratified by class, Leonard Thompson aimed to cater for everyone. The Casino's ground floor offered a main restaurant, first-class restaurant and novel snack bar with soda fountain.

Seaside food was the cause of perennial complaint. Writing for *The Architectural Review* in 1936, Peter Maitland bemoaned the 'genteel teashop in the side street, where you have neither the view of the sea you have come to enjoy nor enough to eat, and where all the gaps are filled with mustard and cress'.[20] Improved menus in attractive settings were therefore a priority for forward-looking resorts. The most extraordinary modern seaside café was

PLEASURE BEACH.

NOAH'S ARK.

CASINO & PLEASURE BEACH.

BLACKPOOL PLEASURE BEACH

PLEASURE BEACH.

ICE DROME

K.203Q

THE CASINO AND PLEASURE BEACH, BLACKPOOL.   H.2287

The Pleasure Beach Casino building includes a manager's
flat which survives with original Emberton furnishings.

The Labworth Café at Canvey Island was
Ove Arup's first solo commission, in 1932–3.

Nardini Lounge, Cafe and Restaurant, Largs

7344X

Milk bars and ice cream parlours proliferated between the wars. Nardini's in Largs opened in 1935 and has become a Scottish seaside institution.

also one of the earliest, built to the designs of Ove Arup in 1932–3. Overlooking the Thames Estuary, the Labworth Café (page 81) was built at Canvey Island, then Britain's fastest-growing seaside resort due to its popularity with holidaymakers from London's East End. As an interwar plotland Canvey was somewhat ramshackle, but the freedom from normal resort regulation allowed Arup to try out radical ideas inspired by Le Corbusier. The site on the sea wall dropped steeply at the rear so Arup designed his café as two drums floating on slender concrete piles. The larger upper drum was glazed around its perimeter, oversailing the promenade and two curved wings that provided seafront shelters. Later works to create more resilient flood defences have sadly concealed the rear structural supports, but with the wings now enclosed for extra dining space the restored Labworth continues in business.

In 1935 the Ayrshire town of Largs got not one but two seafront eateries. Nardini's (opposite) was designed by C Davidson & Sons as a milk-based roadhouse with shops, a café and restaurant. Architectural historian Charles McKean described it as serving 'plentiful dairy ice cream in a vigorous white building which seemed plastered with the stuff'.[21] Italian-owned and art deco-styled ice cream parlours emerged as a seaside staple of the era and Nardini's remains one of the best. Another Italian, Mr Castelvecchi, invested £15,000 in The Moorings (page 84), a 'super-café' by architect James Houston. Designed to attract visitors coming by ferry from Arran, it was itself shaped like a boat with porthole details and the corner cut away to read like the prow of a ship. A thousand dancers once whirled around the rooftop ballroom but the loss of holiday business and damage to its steel frame led to demolition in 1989.

Cafés integrated into other building types provided important income streams and that was particularly so at open-air pools, where it was a well-proven fact that spectators far outnumbered swimmers. In August 1931 *Reynold's Illustrated News* declared that Scotland had 'suddenly gone bathing mad – community bathing mad'. Queues were reported at recently opened 'ponds', as they were called locally, and at Prestwick the new facility was credited with stemming the tide of visitors to English resorts, with accommodation at a premium and the town 'full to overflowing'. Small wonder then that nearly £100,000 was collectively projected for ponds at Ayr, Saltcoats, Largs, Rothesay

The Moorings Café was designed to look like the
prow of a ship facing the waterfront at Largs.

6220.   MORECAMBE, CENTRAL PROMENADE.   AERO PICTORIAL LTD.
136 REGENT STREET, W. 1

Morecambe's modern promenade could boast a renewed
Central Pier, the most expensive lido of the era and the
influential Midland Hotel (bottom right).

Kent's largest open air pool was built
below the cliffs at Ramsgate.

and Millport.[22] By the mid-1930s seaside lidos had reached epic proportions. Scotland's largest opened at Portobello near Edinburgh in 1936, designed by Ian Warner with city engineer William Macartney. It was the first in Britain to have a wave machine, and thanks to its location next to a power station had the rare privilege of heated water. Its most sophisticated architectural element was the cantilevered roof of the west grandstand, which could effortlessly shelter a crowd of up to 2,000. Portobello's café employed a more comfortably safe version of art deco, stepped symmetrically either side of a square clock face and rendered in cream with green tile banding. A similar design appeared at New Brighton's 1934 Bathing Pool, one of the biggest ever built in Britain, covering 4.5 acres at the northern tip of the Wirral Peninsula. The rather more streamlined cream and green café there overlooked an artificial beach on the flat side of a vast D-shaped pool. The work of borough architect G Wilkinson, its interior was flooded with natural light from a barrel-vaulted ceiling of 'glasscrete' bricks.

Lido spending peaked at £130,000 for the grandiosely titled 1936 Super Swimming Stadium, a key element in

Morecambe's modernized seafront, as seen from the air in the postcard on page 85. Kenneth Cross and Cecil Sutton enclosed the 120m (396ft)-long bathing area with curved end colonnades. A two-storey entrance block faced across the water to a café and raked seating for the galas, aquashows and, later, Miss Great Britain beauty contests, for which the lido became famous. Kent's largest open-air pool at Ramsgate (opposite) also maximized its potential for entertainment. Built in 1934–5 and run by Marina Pools and Café Ltd, an offshoot of the Tomson & Wotton Brewery, it was unusual for being a commercial venture. The need for profitability meant architect J H Somerset included extra facilities in the £40,000 scheme, including an attached boating pool at the eastern end. A two-storey building to the west curved towards the sea in a semi-circular bay, offering daily comedy performances in its Solar Café, with dances in its Aero Café ballroom.

Perhaps the most daring modernist structures linked to the fashion for lidos were diving stages. At Scarborough, the South Bay Bathing Pool was updated in 1934 with a 10m (33ft)-high concrete stage angled as if it were a stairway into the clouds. The most iconic diving stage, however, was unveiled at Weston-super-

One of the era's most elegant concrete structures was the diving platform at Weston-super-Mare's 1937 swimming pool.

Mare (opposite) three years later. Here the exquisitely engineered platform used two parallel reinforced-concrete arches as the basis for three tiers of symmetrical boards, with a final board mounted above the apogee of the curve. Such was its structural beauty that it became a symbol for the resort in poster and brochure advertising, raising H A Brown's otherwise conservative lido design to national fame. In 1982 a highly contentious decision allowed demolition of the listed diving stage on health and safety grounds.

The first interwar lido to be given the statutory protection of listing in 1987 was at Saltdean (pages 90–91), near Brighton. Designed by R W H Jones for the Saltdean Estate Company, its status as a progeny of the De La Warr Pavilion was recognized from the time it opened in July 1938. Though small by comparison with others of the period, its pool was hugged by two wings of ground-floor changing rooms topped with sun terraces. At their centre a glazed first-floor café curved elegantly out to greet the water, supported on slim concrete piers. In recent years a full restoration has seen it return to use.

In the West Country, two open-air pools managed to survive, both built out into the sea. Plymouth may not register as a

THE LIDO, SALTDEAN

Saltdean Lido with its original tiered diving stage. The
pool closed in 1940 after only two summer seasons.

The Lido, Saltdean.

ET.4725

The refurbished Saltdean Lido finally re-opened in 1964. On the
brow of the hill is the Ocean Hotel, also designed by R W H Jones.

Jubilee Pool in Penzance is
unique for its triangular shape.

seaside resort today but the council was desperate to encourage visitors in the 1930s, spending some £300,000 on upgrading the front below the Hoe with bathing accommodation, colonnades and the semi-circular Tinside Pool of 1935, by J S Wibberley. In the same year Captain Frank Latham, borough engineer at Penzance in Cornwall, oversaw construction of the Jubilee Pool (opposite) that allowed safe swimming in Mount's Bay whatever the tide. It is unique for its triangular shape, but Latham used great artistry to mediate between the right angles of the actual pool and the larger superstructure, which is bounded by gracefully arced walls said to be inspired by the open wings of a sea gull.

Advances in concrete technology underpinned the era of mega-lidos and it was in the 1933 St Leonards Bathing Pool that the material was allowed to speak in its most uncompromising form. Borough engineer Sidney Little, known locally as the 'concrete king', experimented with his own recipe, using uncrushed shingle from the beach as aggregate, and eschewing any superfluous decoration in a £60,000 lido that was nearly as big as Blackpool's. In a starkly rectilinear building, tiered seating edged the landward side of the 100m (330ft)-long swimming pool. Behind the diving stage, there was a covered promenade with segmental arches framing an upper storey of sliding glass screens overlooking the beach. The postcard on page 94 shows visitors exercising on the roof-level sun deck, which supplemented an indoor gymnasium below the seating area. The building must have seemed an astonishing interloper amid the surrounding Victorian terraces but Little was employed to overhaul Hastings' staid reputation and attract a younger generation. Even if his lido is now gone, the £3 million Little spent improving the seafront between Hastings and St Leonards makes it an important landmark in seaside modernism. To alleviate high local unemployment, most of the work was undertaken by direct labour, including the 457m (1,500ft) covered promenade that updated Blackpool's example from the previous decade. Begun in autumn 1933, it took six months and 42,000 tonnes of concrete to create 'Bottle Alley', so-called because the rear wall features pre-cast panels studded with coloured waste glass that bear archaeological witness to long-lost products and manufacturers. The three semi-circular bastions jutting out to provide integrated shelters can be seen in the postcard on page 95. On the top

SWIMMING POOL, PENZANCE

KPE 102

PHYSICAL DRILL AT THE BATHING POOL ST. LEONARDS-ON-SEA

Physical Training, or PT, was a popular mass pastime
in the 1930s so Sidney Little created space for it
on the flat roofs of his St Leonards Bathing Pool.

HASTINGS, LOWER PROMENADE

78016

Double-decker promenades like 'Bottle Alley' at Hastings
provided extra space for walking and a covered option for
inclement weather.

Midland Hotel, Morecambe.

9509

The sleek curves of Morecambe's
newly built Midland Hotel.

promenade further shelters display some highly original design ideas, those alongside Eversfield Place spanning a change in level down to the roadside, their upper and lower seats backed by coloured confetti-effect panels. Elsewhere, New Brighton has retained its streamlined, flat-roofed shelters; Cromer's cliff path, north of the pier, features moderne, mushroom-like shelters with flat circular roofs at each zig and zag of its progress.

At the other end of the constructional scale were the hotels and apartment blocks that promised a much-needed upgrade in accommodation standards. Investment had been sluggish in the 1920s but Victorian grand hotels, once run by an army of cheap labour, were now putting wealthy visitors off staying at the seaside. In 1932–3 the Midland Hotel at Morecambe showed a way forward, replacing two Victorian establishments run by the London, Midland and Scottish Railway (LMS). On an enviably unhindered site, architect Oliver Hill worked with the curve of the promenade to design a hotel with 40 bedrooms over three floors. Visually arresting and a complete contrast to everything around it, the building was praised for its simplicity. The ground-floor café was an early example of a glazed

drum and on its inner wall husband and wife artists Eric Ravilious and Tirzah Garwood painted a fantasy seaside in night and day. Unfortunately, the pressured schedule meant the plaster was still wet and by 1935 their mural had to be removed; a version of it was recreated in 2013. The sweep of the hotel's landward façade is strikingly captured in the postcard opposite, showing how the curve of the southern corner echoed the bowed stair tower of the central entrance. This was ornamented outside and in by sculptor Eric Gill, who carved two giant seahorses at roof level with a ceiling medallion of Neptune and Triton as the centrepiece of the elegant spiral staircase. Gill did other interior work alongside Denis Tegetmeier, Marion Dorn and Edward Bawden, their employment demonstrating Hill's commitment to the hotel as a work of art in its widest sense.

Other visions of luxury seaside accommodation followed, though not always in conventional hotel form. On a tight corner site along Brighton's built-up seafront, the 1935–6 Embassy Court (page 98) soared above its Regency and Victorian neighbours, to offer 72 apartments over 11 floors. As in his earlier Isokon block of flats, at Lawn Road in Hampstead, Canadian architect

At Embassy Court, Brighton, architect Wells Coates made continuous balconies integral to the building's structure.

1061 **EMBASSY COURT, BRIGHTON**
BEST POSITION ON SEA FRONT
SEE OVER

Wells Coates designed from the inside out, allowing the structural idea to dictate the building's shape and detailed planning. This functionalist purity did not come cheap; annual rents of between £150 and £500 could buy a small house in the town and a rear servants' entrance made the intended class of occupants clear. Ninth and tenth-floor penthouses were advertised as the first in the country. Above them, a continuous sun terrace made the most of stunning Channel views.

Bournemouth's Palace Court Hotel, under construction around the same time, was a hybrid, combining 70 hotel rooms with flats on the upper floors and a members' club on the first floor. Local architects A J Seal and Partners also had to contend with a tightly bounded site so built up 33.5m (110ft) above pavement level. The postcards left and opposite demonstrate the

The streamlined balconies of
Bournemouth's Palace Court Hotel
were applied to the front elevation.

PALACE COURT HOTEL, BOURNEMOUTH.

difference between International Modernism and home-grown
moderne. Nonetheless, *The Architect and Building News* applauded
the Palace Court Hotel's 'freshness and originality both in
design and planning', noting how the public rooms exuded
modern comfort; the restaurant had gilt walls hung with curtains
in brick-red, black and gold, while the club recreation room
boasted a 'gay colour scheme of scarlet and fawn, gold columns,
chromium-tube radiator grilles and serpentine bar'.[23]

The 1937 rebuild of the Queen's Hotel on Torquay's
harbourfront referenced both of the above buildings but failed
to commit wholeheartedly; behind its white balconies the cream
and gold entrance hall was furnished with sturdy oak furniture.
It was another lesson in market forces, where the owners were
unwilling to push clientele beyond their literal comfort zone.

Sandown's Grand Hotel mixed strips of Crittall
windows and bold chevron decoration with
striped awnings reminiscent of Regency seaside villas.

Advertisements in 1930s guidebooks suggest most established resorts had at least one new hotel that traded on its modernity. Surviving examples, in varying condition, include the 1938 Royal York Hotel at Ryde, with a streamlined façade and Morecambe-inspired entrance tower, and the Grand Hotel at Sandown (opposite), also on the Isle of Wight, which mixed a façade of jazzy-coloured chevron patterns with awnings borrowed from Regency Brighton, by way of Queen Victoria's nearby Osborne House. Tynemouth's Park Hotel combined curvaceous bays with cut-away brick balconies and art deco fins, while the Seabank at Porthcawl imported Hollywood moderne glamour to South Wales with a deep mansard roof of shiny green-glazed pantiles and a deco lantern-lookout at the centre of its Y-shaped plan.

Some of the largest and smartest hotels, however, were built away from resort centres specifically to attract car-drivers. The four-storey white rectangle of Saunton Sands Hotel was planted on the green North Devon coast in 1935 next to a new championship golf course. Near Weymouth, the 1937 Riviera Hotel made its architectural impact by spreading longitudinally across the slopes above Bowleaze Cove. Architect L Stewart Smith created gently curving single-storey wings either side of an art deco entrance tower, with the outer 11 bays given an extra floor to balance the compelling rhythm of arches seen in the postcard on page 102. Saltdean's vast Ocean Hotel by R W H Jones opened in 1938, the same year as his nearby lido. It cost the princely sum of £200,000 and could accommodate up to 600 guests in bedroom blocks terraced over a sloping site either side of the hotel's own swimming pool. The design aimed at a sustainable year-round business that allowed whole sections to be mothballed out of season; public rooms were housed in the curved entrance building along with enough bedrooms for winter occupancy. In 1951 the Ocean Hotel was bought by Butlin's and the surviving upper section is now converted to flats.

Embassy Court proved that urban apartment buildings could be successfully transplanted to the seafront and others followed in its wake, notably Argyll Court at Southend's smart suburb of Westcliff-on-Sea, and Osborne Court, overlooking the fashionable yachting centre of Cowes on the Isle of Wight. The most grandiloquent was Marine Court at St Leonards (page 103),

GRAND HOTEL, SANDOWN, ISLE OF WIGHT

BOWLEAZE FROM THE ROAD.

H.333

With no constraint on space the Riviera Hotel could
stretch above Bowleaze Cove near Weymouth.

Marine Court, St. Leonards-on-Sea.

The scale of Marine Court made it
the ultimate example of a liner on land.

The Sun Court at the centre of Prestatyn holiday camp was surrounded by crisp white buildings and enlivened by brightly striped parasols.

which at 14 storeys was the tallest residential building in Britain when it opened in 1938. Architects Kenneth Dalgliesh and Roger K Pullen provided more than a hundred flats and two magnificent restaurants that could seat up to a thousand people. Residents enjoyed luxury hotel service with the amenities of a modern block of flats in a £400,000 building that looked like an ocean liner. Just in case its debt to the *Queen Mary* passed anyone by, the owners borrowed a 7.3m (24ft)-long model of that vessel from Cunard-White Star Line to display in the entrance hall. For the mammoth 1936 San Remo Towers at Boscombe, architect Hector O Hamilton took a uniquely different approach. His rectilinear blocks combine a yellowish-pink brick with stucco on the ground and top floors, where the paired windows have rounded heads. Terracotta roofs and colourful tiled ornament in red, yellow, blue and green mix Italian Renaissance and Spanish Hacienda styles in an overall design that is more California than Dorset.

Another 1930s accommodation alternative was the planned resort. The best-known speculative estate was at Frinton-on-Sea, where development of a 200-acre site on the edge of Essex's most genteel seaside town was overseen by architect Oliver Hill from 1934. Around a central avenue, 1,100 houses were to be zoned according to style, with purchasers on the best 30 acres given a list of architects to choose from that contained the cream of British modernism including Wells Coates, Mendelsohn and Chermayeff, Connell, Ward & Lucas, Joseph Emberton and Maxwell Fry. In the end only around 40 houses were built, about a dozen of them designed by Hill himself. At Churston Ferrers, near Paignton in Devon, the number was even smaller, a cluster of seven striking properties designed by American modernist William Lescaze being all that survive of the Dartington Trust's ambitious 1935 plan for a clifftop resort. Almost contemporary with these projects was the construction of Billy Butlin's first holiday camp on the edge of Skegness in Lincolnshire.

Far less pure, and almost beneath contempt as far as the architectural press was concerned, it was nevertheless framed as an 'Ultra-Modern Development'. Its scale was unprecedented and a reporter for the *Skegness News* described the finished effect in 1936 as 'a vast estate – a veritable township of cool white buildings, tiny houses and exquisite gardens'.[24] Selling

PRESTATYN HOLIDAY CAMP.

W.1801

PRESTATYN HOLIDAY CAMP, BARNACLE BAY

85669

William Hamlyn designed rows of
flat-roofed chalets at Prestatyn.

affordable luxury, Billy Butlin gave the British public just the right
amount of modernistic design, confining flat-roofed buildings
to communal use and accommodating guests in mock-Tudor
'Elizabethan' chalets. His immediate success showed a much
sounder grasp of popular taste than was sadly the case at Frinton
and Churston Ferrers. The all-inclusive package of bed, board
and entertainments offered by holiday camps met a growing
desire for a different seaside experience. The most architecturally
acclaimed 'Chalet village by the sea' was jointly funded by
the LMS and Thomas Cook travel agents among the dunes at
Prestatyn (page 105) on the North Wales coast. Around a central
Sun Court, LMS architect William Hamlyn gave the dining room,
ballroom, ship-shaped bar and flat-roofed chalet lines (opposite)
a coherent modern look that seemed to bode well for expansion
of this camp into a nationwide chain. By the time Prestatyn
opened in 1939 the clouds of conflict were on the horizon and
with Hitler's invasion of Poland that September, the dream of
leisure for all had to be put on hold.

3

FESTIVAL STYLE AT THE SEASIDE

The outbreak of war brought an immediate halt to seaside holidays as well as to a frenetic decade of resort development. From May 1940 an exclusion zone was created along most of the south and east coasts, placing them out of bounds to all but service personnel. Beaches were mined and barbed wire wound along seafronts. Fifty-three piers were requisitioned and intentionally breached, with huge gaps cut in their decks to prevent landing by enemy invaders; some would never be rebuilt. Safely away from the action, Blackpool and other North West resorts remained open throughout the war, but Channel towns were on the front line and suffered badly. Margate was hit by more than 2,700 bombs and shells, destroying 238 buildings and damaging nearly 9,000 others. Prewar it offered a choice of 240 hotels; only two were open in August 1943.

When hostilities ended, the huge job of clearing up began. Pent-up demand saw record numbers flock to the coast as the impact of prewar legislation, combined with full employment, ensured up to 12 million workers were newly entitled to paid holidays. Reconstruction efforts everywhere were hindered by continued rationing and shortages of labour and materials, but the swift rebuilding of Margate Winter Gardens in 1947 was a recognition of just how important the pressure valve of mass leisure was to maintaining popular morale after the conflict.

This Edwardian building had been used as a reception centre for Dunkirk casualties before its east end was reduced to rubble in a bombardment. Stanley Ramsey was commissioned to repair and upgrade the concert hall, employing muralist Mary Adshead to brighten up the bar with a decorative map of Kent. Continuity with 1930s trends was evident in published schemes to build ambitious new seaside attractions yet currents in modernism *were* shifting. The decisive event for the seaside, as for much municipal architecture, was the 1951 Festival of Britain.

A century after the epoch-making Great Exhibition of 1851, the Festival of Britain sought to promote postwar recovery and showcase national advances in science, manufacturing and the arts. A multitude of local events were planned, with the national centrepiece constructed on London's South Bank. Here the architecture of the thematic pavilions was as much part of the exhibition as the buildings' contents, with the overall style determined by director general Gerald Barry and director of architecture Hugh Casson. For young architects whose careers had been put on hold during the war, taking part was a formative experience. As well as cutting-edge structures like the Skylon and the Dome of Discovery, there was an imperative colour and cheer that lifted the South Bank above the lingering dreariness of war-torn towns and cities. Swedish influence, which had been discernible before the war, now increased because, unlike in

Previous page Two of Seaburn's 'super kiosks'. **Below** Even aspects of seafront landscaping, like these primary-coloured ball railings at Cleethorpes, referenced the Festival of Britain.

The new Fountain and Pier, Cleethorpes

C.4321

The Welsh Miami Beach amusement park
opened at Aberavon in 1963 with a sign based
on the South Bank 'abacus' screen of 1951.

most of Europe, the country's neutrality meant modernism had
continued to evolve throughout the 1940s. Around the Festival
site, lessons from Scandinavia were filtered through a revised
vision of the 18th-century picturesque that was self-consciously
English and gently eccentric. Critics later dismissed the 'flimsy'
architecture it spawned – the boxy towers, mixing of colours,
textures and materials, the shallow butterfly roofs, wave-profile
canopies, steep diagonals and glass façades of curtain walling. Yet
for a whole generation of Britons, the Festival style epitomized
what it meant to be modern and its impact on popular taste
explains why it worked so well at the seaside. A perceived lack
of seriousness was hardly a problem when the principal goal of
seaside architecture was to transmit a sense of holiday playfulness
and provide a light-hearted backdrop distinct from the everyday.
The famous grid of bright suspended balls in the South Bank
'abacus' screen by Edward Mills, for example, was referenced
in the shelters along Ventnor's Royal Victoria Pier (1955), in the
railings surrounding the new fountain at Cleethorpes (page 111)
(1962) and the entrance to Miami Beach funfair (opposite) at
Aberavon (1963). None of these were architecturally distinguished

Stairways in the right middle ground of this
postcard led to a series of short 'piers' as
part of the Festival of Britain's Seaside section.

but they expressed a mid-century modern mood that was also conveyed through the graphic design of resort brochures and advertising.

On the South Bank site and upstream at the Battersea Pleasure Gardens, the Festival of Britain acknowledged the importance of coastal resorts in the nation's island sense of identity. The circuit around the South Bank ended at the Seaside Section in front of the Royal Festival Hall, where a series of short 'piers', visible in the postcard opposite, projected over the Thames. Theme convener Anthony Hippisley Coxe realized that visitors would be flagging by the time they arrived and set out to raise a smile with donkey rides and demonstrations of seaside-rock making. There was a giant bucket painted with comic postcard-type illustrations and, under the canvas roof, sunhats and umbrellas were turned into decorative hanging sculptures as a comment on the vagaries of British holiday weather. Barbara Jones, the artist and pioneer of folk-art appreciation, designed the Coastline of Britain display, while Eric Brown and Peter Chamberlin presented a stylized seafront described by *The Illustrated London News* as 'a medley of Victorian boarding-houses,

elegant Regency façades, ice-cream parlours and public-houses'.[25] The press and public lapped it up but resorts themselves were not pleased, particularly since they looked set to lose a significant number of visitors as a result of competition from the Festival. Worthing's publicity officer criticized the lack of people in the seaside model, which he said resembled a town struck by the plague. It was all so far from the modern marketing exercise that the Association of Health and Holiday Resorts had hoped for that they made a formal complaint.

As a waterfront park with amusements and daring rides imported from America, the Battersea Pleasure Gardens revelled in a sort of urban seaside-ness that referenced London predecessors Vauxhall and Cremorne Gardens, with a splash of Brighton on top. There was a boating lake, regular Punch and Judy performances and nightly illuminations. The Grand Vista that represented the key formal element was the combined work of artist John Piper and cartoonist Osbert Lancaster, both of whom had explored the seaside's distinctive landscape in prewar publications. Members of the public more used to enjoying this sort of whimsical fantasy by the sea would have recognized the

SEASIDE   South Bank Exhibition   Festival of Britain 1951

Opposite One of the brightly coloured Guinness travelling clocks on the promenade at Morecambe.

Right The original Festival Clock design on display at Great Yarmouth.

allusions to Regency Brighton or what William Feaver described as a mix of 'Fonthill Abbey and Southend Pier.'[26] When it came to building the crowd-pleasing Far Tottering and Oyster Creek Railway, *Punch* artist Rowland Emmett collaborated with Harry Barlow of Southport, who had built miniature passenger railways for various northern resorts.

This was not the only example of graphic design turned into flamboyant three dimensions. Guinness employed the Lewitt-Him partnership to incorporate the toucan, and other animals from its advertising campaign, into a 7.6m (25ft)-high Festival Clock that gave a show of moving figures every quarter-hour. So many requests were made to borrow it that Guinness commissioned eight travelling clocks. Until they were finally withdrawn in 1966 these toured resorts including Morecambe (opposite), Southend, Paignton, Barry Island, South Shields, Hastings, Great Yarmouth (right), Cleethorpes, Clacton and Brighton, extending memories of Festival year for thousands of holidaymakers.

Countrywide Festival participation encompassed pageants, exhibitions, commemorative clocks and new bus stops. Ramsgate Council organized a summer-long Festival of Light featuring

GUINNESS CLOCK, GT. YARMOUTH.

The 1951 entrance to
Eastbourne Pier.

three purpose-built concrete fountains with colour-changing illuminations. The sole surviving fountain in Victoria Gardens, which looks like it could have come from an interwar lido, is now Grade II listed. Skegness borough engineer Rowland Jenkins, who had done so much to transform the seafront since the 1920s, added one last amenity before his retirement. His 1951 Festival Centre was an outdoor auditorium intended for dancing, roller skating and sporting displays. Eastbourne's Festival contribution had been on the drawing board since 1946 when S G Scales made his first designs for a new pier entrance. The postcard opposite shows the curved kiosks finally completed in 1951, crowned with a clock and decorative grilles that still had a deco moderne feel. The Pier Company chairman described it as 'one of the most artistically streamlined reinforced concrete jobs in the country'.[27] Streamlining was still in evidence at Brighton too, where a new brick bathing pavilion formed part of wider Festival celebrations. Like its curved design, the concept of council changing rooms was soon outdated, and in 1957 the building was converted into a milk bar. After the South Bank site closed and the prospect of demolition loomed, the mayor of Brighton hatched a much bolder commemoration

plan. The Festival idea had originated with Labour politicians and, though it was a Conservative government that saw it through to completion, they had no desire to keep it open or even keep anything other than the Royal Festival Hall standing. Sensing an opportunity, Brighton's mayor proposed that his town salvage the Dome of Discovery designed by Ralph Tubbs. The council needed a new conference venue and considered the plan in spring 1952, sadly concluding that there was no obvious place to erect what was then the world's largest aluminium structure.

In the postwar period coastal decision-making had to steer an increasingly fine line between the needs of visitors and expanding residential communities. Yet the speed of recovery was actually remarkable. In August 1952 *Daily Herald* columnist Hannen Swaffer reported from the country's four leading resorts. At Blackpool he found around 8 million people, mostly workers, were visiting every year. The town had bedspace for 300,000 visitors, to whom it offered a choice of 14 live shows, the widest range outside London. Brighton welcomed 200,000 staying guests over the four-month season who contributed £2 million annually to the town's economy, bolstered by an additional 1.2 million day

Ventnor Pier re-opened in
1955 with Festival-inspired
shelters along its deck.

and weekend trippers. Scarborough, he suggested, 'where fashion formerly flaunted itself, is making itself more and more part of the welfare state'. Municipal entertainments brought in £130,000 a year while the council's catering department had a turnover of £120,000. As Swaffer discovered, 'a British seaside town of any size is Big Business'. From its wartime low, Margate was now offering accommodation at 1,250 establishments capable of sleeping 200,000 people. The council kept profits in the town by running visitor attractions and food outlets and during the 1952 season expected to sell 2.25 million tickets for deckchair hire.[28]

This revival did not immediately translate into new buildings. Ambition usually predated the necessary government sanction for loans and building licences and it was not until austerity conditions ended in the mid-1950s that improvement projects could begin. Around the same time, living standards began to rise: between 1955 and 1969, average weekly earnings increased by 130 per cent. People who had famously 'never had it so good' were also, from 1953, entitled to a minimum of two weeks' paid holiday. One upshot was a growing demand for foreign destinations. Nevertheless, the number of Britons going abroad was still dwarfed by the domestic market which, throughout the 1960s, was estimated by the British Travel Association to account for around 30 million holidays annually, compared to only around 5 million overseas.[29] This did not mean resorts could rest on their interwar laurels and expect people to come just because they always had. Those places unwilling or unable to update their attractions would come to regret it later.

The totemic status of pleasure piers had yet to be challenged. Indeed, Alderman Benwell of Boscombe memorably declared in 1955, 'A seaside without a pier is like a pig without ears.'[30] Wartime damage created the conditions for a new phase of reinvention. Ventnor's Royal Victoria Pier was condemned in 1948 but a 90 per cent government grant meant the council could begin reconstruction in early 1951. After the 30m (100ft) breach was filled, the pier head was widened and reinforced for a new bandstand and cafeteria designed by local architect Basil Phelps, completed in 1955. The modernistic open-air arena was reminiscent of Weymouth's 1939 Bandstand Pier but the Festival-inspired screen shelters, seen along the deck in the postcard opposite, were more in tune with the pier's Calypso Coffee Bar,

The spartan concrete design
of Deal's post-war pier.

an espresso pioneer on the Isle of Wight, just three years after the
first Gaggia machine appeared in London.

A more decisive break with past pier structures came at
Deal (opposite) in 1957. The Kent resort's former iron pier of
1863 was one of the earliest built by Victorian marine engineer
Eugenius Birch. In January 1940 it was rent in two by a drifting
vessel. Later that year, Winston Churchill ordered demolition
of the residue to give clear sight lines for coastal gunners. The
council's strategy for a staged rebuilding was rejected by central
government in 1950, but removal of the surviving Birch tollbooths
in 1954 signalled the commencement of work by Concrete Piling
Ltd, to the designs of consultant engineers William Halcrow &
Partners. Elain Harwood encapsulated the look of the resulting
structure when she called Deal 'the austerity pier – no frills, just a
gawky charm in its angled pairs of concrete piers and bus station
entrance'.[31] Continuous bench seating along the 312m (1,026ft)
length followed the precedent of the old pier, with a series of
kinks in its functional deck provided by glazed shelters oversailing
the edge. In 2008 a competition-winning café designed by Niall
McLaughlin gave the pier head a fittingly sparse new focus.

On the south coast, the sister resorts of Bournemouth
and Boscombe saw their piers revived at different speeds
under the same borough engineer and architect's departments.
Contractors quickly bridged the wartime gap in the 1880
Eugenius Birch pier at Bournemouth and the public returned from
November 1947. Historically, Boscombe had always come second,
its 1889 pier failing to compete with that of its bigger neighbour
and ultimately being taken over by Bournemouth Corporation
in 1904. Fifty years later, members of the Boscombe Ratepayers
Association were told their derelict pier might never be rebuilt,
so government funding in 1955 came as a welcome surprise.
An entirely new concrete pier (page 124) was begun in November
1957, employing a different method from that at Deal. Here the
neck was supported on seven groups of pre-stressed concrete
piles of alternating long and short spans. The entrance building
(page 125) also had a striking verve. Completed in 1960, its slim
boomerang roof floated over kiosks, lavatories and shelters built
in a mid-century mix of materials including smooth cream and
blue tiles, craggy natural stone and dark teak. A hall at the end of
the pier, known as The Mermaid, opened for roller skating in 1962.

THE PIER, BOSCOMBE

Boscombe's rebuilt pier used pre-stressed concrete piles.

A thin concrete roof floats over
the 1960 entrance to Boscombe Pier.

Bournemouth Pier Theatre with
colourful coin-in-the-slot bathing huts
in the foreground.

This was a smaller version of the theatre added to
Bournemouth Pier in 1960, both of them worked on by local-
born architect Elisabeth Scott, the first woman to win a national
architecture competition with her 1928 design for rebuilding the
Shakespeare Memorial Theatre at Stratford-upon-Avon. Scott
returned home to Bournemouth during the war, taking a job
with A J Seal and Partners, architects for the Palace Court Hotel,
before becoming assistant to the borough architect John Burton.
Bournemouth Pier Theatre (opposite) updated the 'building as
boat' conceit, with raked timber supports adding rhythm and
colour either side of the curved roof and a 'bridge' with glazed
captain's nest at the back of the fly tower, from where the pier
master supervised the comings and goings of pleasure steamers.
In 2013 the 690-seat concert hall was converted to an activity
centre, but the circular sea-end café still serves diners under its
self-supporting and stunning quilt-effect shallow dome.

Towers helped give other pier buildings a distinctive mid-
century quality. The South Pier at Lowestoft lost its 1890s Arts
and Crafts-style pavilion to wartime bombing. On 2 May 1956, the
Duke of Edinburgh opened its multi-purpose replacement (pages

LW 8   LOWESTOFT. SOUTH PIER AND TOWER

Large areas of glazing along the first floor and in the observation
tower were used to offset the blank upper walls of the new
concert hall on Lowestoft's South Pier.

A yellow wall below the South Pier tower added extra interest
to the mixed façades at Lowestoft.

Symbols of modernity – curtain walling,
advanced concrete roofing and the new
hovercraft at Southsea Pier.

128 and 129) by Norwich architects Eric Skipper and
R B Corless. Based on a lightweight steel box, the building's load
rested on the pile positions of a renewed concrete substructure.
Its 18m (60ft)-high observation tower, with staircases visible
through glazed walls, recalled that of the New Schools Pavilion at
the Festival of Britain designed by Maxwell Fry and Jane Drew.
The gently curved roof of the concert space made passing
reference to the Royal Festival Hall, while jutting angles and a
pop of citrus yellow on the beach elevation suggested further
inspiration from the South Bank. Clarence Pier's circular iron and
glass pavilion at Southsea was another casualty of war, destroyed
during an air raid in January 1941. Twenty years elapsed before
a new building opened on 1 June 1961, exactly a century after
its predecessor. Portsmouth architects A E Cogswell and
R Lewis Reynish managed to 'catch the mood of holiday gaiety' in
a primary-coloured triumph of bar and restaurant blocks, either
side of an angular pebbledashed tower capped with a round
viewing deck. The restaurant's distinctive wave profile seen in the
postcard opposite came courtesy of a thin concrete roof slab that
took strength from its concertina shape. This allowed the walls

to be built as 'great window frames of anodized aluminium partly
filled in with glass and partly with panels of vitreous enamelled
steel in bright red and yellow'. Curtain walling on the bar block
featured blue vitreous panels, and there was a second, smaller
tower over the staff staircase and goods lift. As the *Portsmouth
Evening News* proudly reported, this was 'another piece of
advanced reinforced concrete engineering – four warped shells
of a shape called a hyperbolic paraboloid, standing together and
supported only in the middle of each of the four sides.' The top
surface of these extraordinary wings originally gleamed gold in
the sun; the undersides were painted bold red and white stripes.[32]
Today the complex is all yellow and blue, still a vibrant enticement
to the funfair that takes up the rest of the pier.

No less dramatic is the Douglas Sea Terminal (pages 132
and 133), which has welcomed passengers to the Isle of Man since
1965. Elain Harwood called it a 'glorious cake stand of a building',
the witty Crow's Nest Restaurant perched at the centre of a
three-legged plan a real accomplishment, managing simultaneously
to celebrate its maritime purpose, the Manx symbol *and* a seaside
playfulness.[33] The firm of Davidson Marsh took over the project

Sea Terminal, Douglas, Isle of Man.　　　　RT.348

The central feature of Douglas Sea Terminal is affectionately known as the Lemon Squeezer.

The Sea Terminal remains a key entry point to the Isle of Man
with sweeping curves that embrace the visitor.

The three-storey building below Great Yarmouth Tower featured an ice rink, amusements and shops at street level, with the Oasis Restaurant and Tower Ballroom on the floors above.

from T H Kennaugh, who had been given the original commission to replace an 1889 building on the Victoria Pier. With boats bringing a steady stream of tourists from England, Ireland, Scotland and Wales this was never a pleasure pier but its new terminal promised pleasant surroundings in a large ground-floor waiting hall with sun lounge and buffet. The affectionately dubbed Lemon Squeezer on top gets its multi-gabled roofline from a frame of Omnia beams, made of concrete reinforced with a steel lattice structure, out of which a concrete spike pokes skyward. Across the façades, crushed glass in the blue and white mineralite wall panels gives the building extra sparkle.

One further observation deck worthy of mention was built atop the 1965 Oasis Tower (opposite) on Great Yarmouth's Marine Parade. Its designer had evidently been keeping an eye on transport innovations because the octagonal viewing gallery had distinct echoes of the contemporary Pennine Tower at Forton services on the M6 motorway, itself based on the design of airport control towers. At Great Yarmouth the shaft of the tower lit up like a lamp at night. Below it, three floors of entertainments were differentiated across the façade by stripes of blue and yellow

The 1960 Weymouth Pavilion originally featured panels of mosaic mermaids either side of the main entrance.

vitreous panels. A four-storey hotel block mediated between the breadth of the main building and the height of the tower, featuring angled balconies to the north- and south-facing bedrooms.

Weymouth Pavilion (opposite) has long been overlooked by architectural historians but of all mid-century pier buildings it is the one that best marries seaside precedent with Festival *joie de vivre*. Superseding an Edwardian pavilion known as the Ritz, which burned down in April 1954, construction on the new combined theatre and ballroom began in September 1958 to designs by the London firm of Verity and Beverley. Following the death of lead architect Samuel Beverley in May 1959, the project was completed by his son-in-law Anthony Denny. Prominently located between Weymouth's harbour and the sweep of its sandy bay, the Pavilion took inspiration from the Georgian buildings surrounding it. Tall, fluted pilasters in pebbledash concrete give the entrance front its essential rhythm, the central five bays making a gently curved and glazed bow feature that is delightfully swagged below the copper roof. When the pavilion opened in July 1960 the bays either side were decorated with mosaic mermaids made from locally collected shells and pebbles. Weathering led these to be covered over in

the 1980s, though simpler patterns survive in the lower sections. Another glazed bow turns the corner facing the Georgian terraces of the Esplanade but it is the patterned side walls that will most please enthusiasts of mid-century design. Continuing the building's subtle colour palette, the repeated chain of compressed rectangles and squashed crosses plays with changes in texture and depth, between the smooth cream grid and the rough plaster-pink render, to turn a potentially nondescript elevation into a visual treat.

The only other seaside instance of translating flat wall plane into bold pattern happened at Southend in the Cliffs Pavilion of 1964. This had a long gestation period as prewar work had to be halted then adapted as requirements changed. The completed scheme by borough architect P F Burridge was based around a multi-purpose auditorium, its zigzag roof complemented by a cantilevered butterfly canopy over the combined fly tower and observation deck. The postcard on page 138 demonstrates the graphic impact of the two-tone repeat pattern applied in pre-cast panels above a brick and glass ground floor.

Dunoon lost its waterfront pavilion to fire in 1949; just a year later, they secured a competition-winning design by

A striking use of repeat pattern on the
1964 Cliffs Pavilion at Southend.

Strong colours helped define postwar façades, as seen in the
two shades of blue used at the Queen's Hall, Dunoon.

The 1963 Congress Theatre at Eastbourne is still the largest theatre on the South Coast.

Glasgow architect Ninian R J Johnston to replace it. As funding hit inevitable delays the building became simultaneously more expensive and more necessary. The Dunoon area earned nearly £1 million a year from the tourist trade, making it one of the biggest holiday resorts in Scotland. The problem was that since workers had won the right to longer holidays more of them were travelling south to English resorts. Without a new concert space Dunoon would be unable to compete, but it meant committing a community of just 10,000 people to a £200,000 project. When the Queen's Hall (page 139) opened in April 1958 *The Scotsman* declared it 'one of the most up-to-date of its type in Scotland'; passengers arriving by boat 'doon the watter' were met with a contemporary vision combining blue elevations, curtain walling and a curved Festival-style roof.[34] Sadly this could not halt the virtual collapse of steamer services in the late 1960s, as people chose to drive to alternative holiday destinations. In the 2015–18 Queen's Hall renovation almost all of its Festival gaiety was stripped away.

On England's south coast the Congress Theatre (opposite) at Eastbourne has fared better thanks to the Grade II* listing that ensured sensitive refurbishment in 2019. Early ideas for a new concert and conference hall focused on the seafront but it was for a site in Devonshire Park that Bryan & Norman Westwood & Partners prepared designs in 1958. Built for £450,000, with a two-tier auditorium to seat 1,678 people, it opened five years later. The mixed palette of materials, including several different stone finishes, brick, slate and dark aggregate panels, coupled with extensive double glazing, was considered 'distracting' by the *Architects' Journal,* which wanted to move on from the Royal Festival Hall precedent. *The Stage* took a different view, praising 'An exterior which is striking without being ostentatious; an interior that is so light, spacious and airy that it creates a sense of serenity …'[35] Television had yet to kill off the traditional summer variety season and the Congress became the new home of long-running revue company The Fol-de-Rols.

The postwar popularity of West Country destinations encouraged the neighbouring South Devon resorts of Torquay and Paignton to invest substantial sums in updating their entertainment provision. In 1961, Torquay's £350,000 Princess Gardens Development Scheme, comprising a dual-carriageway

Festival Hall, Paignton

P.0145

Opposite Local architect Cyril Thurley mixed colour and texture in his design for Paignton Festival Hall.

Right Every elevation at Paignton was different, with the theatre entrance on the east side given a glazed façade.

Paignton Festival Hall.

B4K

seafront road, promenade with two-tiered elliptical 'Banjo Pier', café and Princess Theatre, won the 'Come to Britain' trophy for the best new attraction. Borough surveyor F T W Nixon extended the line of the harbour wall on more than a hundred concrete piles to create a platform for the new theatre. This had enough contemporary touches to suggest its modernity but what publicity officer John Robinson called its 'comfortably friendly atmosphere' was really a safe blandness that Paignton enthusiastically rejected in its rival Festival Hall.[36] The designer of that building was local man Cyril Thurley, former president of the Devon and Cornwall Society of Architects, who championed the expertise of regional practices against imported firms 'with high-sounding names'.[36] After four decades of discussion about Paignton's need for a permanent entertainment centre, progress at Torquay provided new impetus and on a prime seafront site Thurley made every elevation count. The postcard views opposite and above show how he combined blue and yellow sections on the west front with chunky local red sandstone and ample glass. Above the roadside

Royal Floral Hall Gardens, Rhyl.

32

Rhyl's tropical glasshouse became known as the Royal Floral Hall after a visit from the Duke and Duchess of Gloucester in June 1960.

entrance a corrugated concrete feature suggested a large seagull had come to rest there while, on the south front facing the beach, a glazed restaurant was cantilevered over the promenade. Critics who disliked Eastbourne's Congress for its mixed monochrome façades would have run a mile from Paignton's potpourri, yet it was unapologetic in embracing the end phase of Festival style, even if that meant building costs had doubled to £400,000 by the time it opened in June 1967. The council owners made a loss almost every year, though that was not unusual at the seaside where packed summer shows were impossible to replicate out of season. In 1999 its mongrel modernity disappeared in a deeply boring conversion to multi-screen cinema use. Two further seaside theatres from the late 1960s remain in operation in the South West: the Mowlam Theatre at Swanage, opened in 1967, and the Weston-super-Mare Playhouse by W S Hattrell & Partners of Coventry, which replaced an earlier structure destroyed by fire in 1969. Neither had the chutzpah of Paignton Festival Hall.

The postwar seaside environment was not just the product of buildings. Teams of council gardeners kept promenades in continual bloom and the vibrant displays of bedding plants captured in so many postcard views now evoke a lost civic pride. On the North Wales coast, Rhyl Urban District Council went one better, investing £21,000 in a 68 × 12m (225 × 40ft) glasshouse that opened as the Floral Hall (opposite) in 1959. Providing indoor vegetation as an all-weather attraction had first been tried in Victorian winter gardens of the 1870s but the postwar context was different; in what the *Liverpool Daily Post* called a high unemployment 'year of stress in Rhyl', the parrots that flew among the tropical plants and cacti of the Floral Hall marked a long-awaited sign of progress and a novel experience for holidaymakers whose incomes could not yet meet their aspirations to foreign travel.[38] Skegness Council investigated the possibility of having its own floral hall and sent a deputation to Rhyl but was unable to proceed, having been stung by the cost of roofing in their 1951 Festival Centre. The open-air venue suffered from inevitable bad-weather cancellations, so in 1963 the new borough surveyor, H M P Cooper, was asked to cover the existing skating rink, quickly and at moderate cost. To maintain an uninterrupted floor area Cooper and consultant engineer Ian Paxton used four intersecting 31m (101ft)-span glulam (glued laminate) arches to

The unique roof shape of Skegness Festival Pavilion was designed to cover an existing skating rink without the use of intermediate supports. It took just two months to build.

support the 'folded plate type of roof' seen in on page 147.[39] It took just two months to erect the renamed Festival Pavilion but the brick side walls and Douglas fir cladding of this strikingly unusual seaside interior doubled the budget to more than £20,000.

For smaller resorts, promenade improvements often represented better value for money. Seaburn emerged as a day-trip destination in the 1920s, but Sunderland Corporation had such grand plans for it to compete with nearby South Shields that in 1946 it produced a £1 million masterplan, which envisaged building the largest theatre in the North of England. Though the economic situation prevented its realization, thousands of visitors came to Seaburn and its classification as an official resort by the Ministry of Food in 1949 meant traders received an additional allocation of rationed sweets to meet holiday demand. Another step forward came with the appointment of Frank Hogg as Entertainment, Publicity and Catering Manager in 1952. Previously employed at Bognor Regis and Folkestone, Hogg came to Seaburn direct from the role of assistant entertainment manager at the Battersea Festival Gardens. His hand can be seen in the seafront enhancements that got underway in 1954 with the relocation of

an existing amusement park to create a series of lawns adorned with ten 'super kiosks'. Candy-coloured and full of Festival Gardens spirit, their stripy circular roofs can be seen in the postcard on page 148, capping jaunty slanted walls. Unfortunately, these kiosks were as short-lived as Seaburn's heyday, but at Littlehampton in West Sussex the 1956 kiosk development still bristles with buckets and spades in the season. This single flat-roofed building incorporates a number of 'walkways' between the different units of its curved structure, along with a small amount of sheltered seating.

Other postwar shelters have had mixed fortunes. The series of shelters and kiosks in the postcard of Rhos-on-Sea promenade (page 149), at Colwyn Bay, were erected in the late 1960s using pebbledash and punctured concrete panels under blue roofs. Turned down for listing, they are gradually being removed for new sea-defence works. Hunstanton's 1963 butterfly shelters, designed by Norwich architect Alec T Wright & Partners, were restored with lottery funding in 2016.

The quirkiest postwar beach huts appeared at Mablethorpe and Sutton-on-Sea, where cast concrete wall panels

The Festival Pavilion and Gardens, Skegness 29

THE PROMENADE, SEABURN, SUNDERLAND

L 7180

The first of ten 'super kiosks' opened at Seaburn, Sunderland, in 1955 selling refreshments such as toffee apples and candy floss. Gypsy Rose Lee told fortunes from one in the 1960s.

Rhos-on-Sea, North Wales.

18

Pierced concrete blocks and pebbledash were combined
under blue roofs in the shelters at Rhos-on-Sea.

were paired with corrugated roofs made from recycled Nissen huts. Lincolnshire's flat landscape was littered with wartime airfields and the salvage they provided gave an exotic, pagoda-like profile to the chalets in the postcard shown opposite. A more widespread trend was for hut blocks built in timber or brick, examples of which survive at Filey in Yorkshire and Felixstowe in Suffolk. The development of Boscombe seafront around its new pier included more than a hundred chalets in a ship-shaped, three-tier structure (page 152), with raked partitions along its top level. Similarities with Bournemouth Pier Theatre were unsurprising since the designs emanated from the same borough architect's office. Yacht and fish motifs decorated the balcony railings when these chalets opened in 1957 but they were removed for safety reasons in the Hemingway Design conversion to 'surf pods' in 2009. Probably the most daring reinvention of the beach-hut form came at Ramsgate's West Undercliff, where during the winter of 1960–61 rotten wooden huts were replaced by prefabricated concrete units that, once fitted together, made a large public shelter with 80 chalets stacked above it in two layers. The postcard on page 153 shows how the recessed ground floor made the chalets appear to float and the effective way in which contrasting grey and yellow paint was used to break up the building's mass. Plans to build a connected restaurant that would rest on piloti over the promenade never came to fruition.

As in previous decades, refreshment venues were quick to take up modernizing trends. Noteworthy new cafés were built but many more were created out of existing buildings thanks to updated fascias, Festival interiors and the installation of a jukebox. Eastbourne's 1961 Wish Tower Café adopted the new 'help yourself' service, causing some misapprehension among older residents who thought it would rule out having afternoon tea with friends. This glazed seafront venue by borough surveyor Raymond Williams was intended as a memorial to townspeople killed in the war. At Westward Ho! the Fairway Buoy brought mid-century modernism to the North Devon coast, combining a triangular plan with full-height glazing, blue and yellow panels, grey brick and porthole windows. Nautical references were perennially popular, as were curved forms that made the most of views. Nowhere was this accomplished better than on the end of Dover's Prince of Wales Pier, where the base of an existing lighthouse was encircled

THE CHALETS, SOUTH END, MABLETHORPE. L.2800.

This block near Boscombe Pier was intended to provide
sheltered space off the promenade for 1,800 beach-goers
with two tiers of rental chalets above.

St. Lawrence Beach, Ramsgate.

ET.4699

Alternating grey and yellow walls enhanced the design of the
pre-fabricated concrete chalets at Ramsgate's West Cliff.

Circular forms and illuminations
in the Pelham Place fountain
and café at Hastings.

with a glazed café raised on concrete piloti to make the 1960
Lighthouse Café. On Hastings seafront the round shape of Iorio
& Di Mascio (opposite), with its upper brick storey set back
behind concrete pillars, provided a good backdrop for postcard
views of the traffic-calming 1960 Pelham Place roundabout and
illuminated fountain. Italian café owners around the coast supplied
holidaymakers with the milky coffee and ice-cream sundaes
that were now expected seaside treats, in spaces that merged
European flavours with the colourful wipe-clean aesthetic of
American diners, all mirror glass, vinyl banquettes and Formica.
Morelli's at Broadstairs is the best-known, not least because it has
built a potent retro brand around its 1957–8 décor. The winged
chrome canopy above its shopfront is redolent of American
automobile design, while in its pink interior, wicker basket chairs
cluster around oval tables with patterned laminate tops. Fans of
Formica should also head to Tophams in Bridlington, Scarborough
Harbour Bar and the Ritz Café at Millport on the Scottish island
of Great Cumbrae. Thankfully these wonderful café interiors
endure while a lack of appreciation for other postwar seaside
buildings has seen many lost or significantly altered.

4

THE BRITISH COSTAS

Festival-style modernism maintained a healthy presence at resorts well into the 1960s but new pressures were simultaneously seeking to reinvent the seaside. Young architects pursuing their utopian dreams formulated brutalism as the next modernist wave. For a while this chimed with hopes that a leisured life for everyone was just around the corner, based on the presumption that sustained economic growth and rising living standards would always continue into the future. In this optimistic forecast, people would work less, making provision for their long leisure hours a political imperative alongside housing, schools and hospitals. Architectural historians Alistair Fair and Otto Saumarez-Smith have recently explored how this view informed the construction of new urban theatres and municipal leisure centres.[40] At the seaside, the fashionable 'leisure centre' designation was broadly applied to cover commercial amusement venues as well as indoor pool attractions funded by local authorities.

In July 1971 a huge complex that sought to integrate both these things opened at Douglas on the Isle of Man. Summerland had the potential to be the De La Warr Pavilion of its day, the entertainment building that set the agenda for seaside development with a new vision and new materials. Inside, the whole giddy gamut of seaside pleasures was brought together. On the entrance floor of the 21m (70ft)-high enclosed Solarium,

traditional end-of-the-pier performers and Punch and Judy played to crowds seated in deckchairs, while holidaymakers on other levels enjoyed restaurants, bars, shops, bingo, arcade games, sporting events and an indoor funfair. On the top floor people lazed on bean bags under sun lamps; there was a discotheque in the basement and a swimming pool next door.

Victorian entrepreneurs had already provided the model for mixed-use indoor attractions. Underneath the 1894 Blackpool Tower, the palatial decoration of the ballroom, menagerie, aquarium, circus, shops, cafés and bars gave Lancashire millworkers the thrill of being transported to an otherwise impossibly grand existence. From the 1960s the suspension of disbelief was built upon the idea of foreign warmth and permanent sunshine. Though the actual exodus was still some time off, the shrewdest resorts set out to create artificial environments as a home-grown answer to the lure of the Spanish Costas. It was the beginning of a creeping rejection of the promenade as the source of all pleasures. Despite foreign competition, industry figures show that domestic tourism was booming into the mid-1970s. In the decade between 1965 and 1975 stay-away holidays in Britain, of a minimum four nights, went up from 30 to 40 million annually. Over the same period, figures for overseas holidays rose from 5 to 8 million.[41] The bigger challenge for 'traditional' resorts came from the domestic trend towards self-catering, camping and caravanning, allied to the growing popularity

Previous page Blackpool Pleasure Beach in the 1960s, with the many-triangled roof of the Derby Racer in the centre and a re-fronted Fun House to its left. **Below** For a while, Penarth Esplanade car park had its own amusement arcade on the lower deck.

Penarth Esplanade

P.3712

of Devon and Cornwall with their long stretches of 'unspoilt' coast, a loaded term for all that it implied about the built-up seaside elsewhere. Since the dawn of the railway age, wealthy visitors had made a habit of moving on as soon as crowds adopted their previously select resorts and mass car ownership now extended that privilege to a wider section of the holidaying public. By 1960, 47 per cent of tourists were driving to their summer destination, with the number of private cars on British roads going steadily upwards from 4 million in 1956 to more than 11 million in 1970.[42] The sad irony was that visitors to quaint South West fishing villages threatened the very tranquil quality they hoped to find. Every place on the coast, big or small, was forced to wrestle with an immense seasonal influx of motor vehicles. The solution attempted at Penarth, on the Glamorgan coast, was a multi-storey car park built out over the beach (page 159). Designed by H D Watkins & Associates with engineer J B Parsons, it opened in 1968 boasting glorious views across the Bristol Channel from its concrete decks. Though a view of the car park itself was issued in postcard form it did not inspire imitations elsewhere.

Grey concrete structures were a sign of the times and high-rise towers audaciously punctured the line of seafront buildings at many resorts. In the mid-1960s even more extensive plans for redevelopment were made than were (thankfully) executed. From 1962 Blackpool Council considered a scheme by Covell, Matthews & Partners to transform the town centre and Golden Mile. Parts of the Civic Centre were built on space left by removal of Central Station in the wake of Beeching's rail cuts but an idea for eight walkways over the road, connecting promenade and beach, was not pursued despite seafront congestion. After the M55 connected Blackpool into the national motorway network in 1975, a pedestrian bridge (opposite) was opened south of the tower, but it was hardly used and became a white elephant.

Chamberlin, Powell and Bon, architects of the Golden Lane Estate and the Barbican in London, produced schemes for Weston-super-Mare in 1961 and Folkestone in 1965. These employed the brutalist forms used inland that were inspired by Le Corbusier's 1952 Unité d'Habitation housing block at Marseilles, which elevated structural concrete to an art form. The stringencies of postwar reconstruction favoured concrete

People kept walking across the seafront road at Blackpool despite construction of a pedestrian bridge from the 1976 Palatine Buildings to the beach.

Chamberlin, Powell and Bon's White Cliffs development at Folkestone influenced the design of seafront flats elsewhere around the coast.

for its rapidity, while technological advances enabled it to morph into shapes and volumes that both challenged nature and retained an integrity of function and materials. In the right hands it did not have to be brutalizing, and the 1972 White Cliffs development of flats and maisonettes actually built by Chamberlin, Powell and Bon on The Leas at Folkestone (opposite) has a design of stepped windows that works well by the sea.

By far the biggest scheme to go ahead covered a 15-acre site behind Brighton seafront. Designed by Russell Diplock Associates, Churchill Square shopping centre, with its associated offices, car parks and tower blocks, was the culmination of a slum clearance programme begun in the 1930s. The first completed element was the most seasidey. In November 1965 the Top Rank Suite opened with a dance hall and bars to which an ice rink and ten-pin bowling alleys were added the following year. Critics hated its windowless walls and failed to appreciate the bold faceted roof made of pale gold anodized aluminium intended to glitter in the sun. They described it as a 'ruff', a 'ham-frill' and a 'barbaric crown', dismissing the eye-catching shapes of what was the latest in a long line of architectural signposts by the sea that went back to onion

The Leas, Folke

F.0453

Bedford Hotel and Sea Front, Brighton.

ET.5438R

Phases of Brighton development: 1930s Embassy Court, 1950s brick bathing pavilion-turned-milk-bar and, towering over all, the 1960s high-rise Bedford Hotel.

domes on Victorian piers. Now the Odeon, it is the sole surviving example of an eclectic trend for geometric roof forms noted later in the chapter. The phased building of the new shopping centre came next, executed in concrete, steel and glass. Writing in 1970, Brighton historian Clifford Musgrave praised the way buildings were linked by a series of open piazzas leading to the seafront, embodying 'some of the best aspects of modern planning, in providing open spaces and features of human scale, removed from motor traffic, between the vast blocks of buildings'.[43] Public opinion in the form of footfall disagreed and, as shops emptied, the decision was taken to rebuild in the mid-1990s. Other elements of the 1960s development included Chartwell Court, one of three projected blocks of flats by Russell Diplock Associates, and two towers by Richard Seifert & Partners, the 24-storey Sussex Heights completed in 1966 behind the Hotel Metropole, and Bedford Towers (opposite), a 17-storey replacement for the neo-classical Bedford Hotel that burned down in 1964.

New hotels were conspicuous by their absence in the immediate postwar period. By the 1960s there was an urgent need for up-to-date accommodation, particularly at the luxury end of the market. The Victorian behemoths that proclaimed their exclusivity in names like the Grand, Imperial and Palace were aging badly, and many would ultimately be lost to the wrecking ball. Others were wholly or partially rebuilt. Extensive renovation of Brighton's Metropole Hotel, designed by the Victorian architect of the Natural History Museum, Sir Alfred Waterhouse, was most evident at roof level where its restive collection of pinnacles, turrets and cupolas was deemed structurally unsound. Richard Seifert & Partners took the opportunity to add new floors and a glamorous Starlit Room restaurant. Much of the hotel's original character disappeared in what was seen as a necessary trade-off for its economic survival.

Eastbourne's Cavendish Hotel took a direct hit from a German bomb in 1942 but it was not until 1965 that a new corner block was added by Fitzroy Robinson & Partners. Following existing window heights, this made play with the relationship between wall and glass, terminating in a flat-roofed penthouse. There was no appetite for pastiche, and marketing postcards (pages 166 and 167) show how important the extension was to the hotel's image. At Torquay, the five-star Imperial promoted itself as 'The English hotel in the

CAVENDISH HOTEL

A 'modern' family pose on Continental loungers in front
of the extended Cavendish Hotel, Eastbourne.

CAVENDISH HOTEL

The same guests pictured in their luxury bedroom
with wrap-around windows and balcony.

Motel Burstin in Folkestone pictured halfway through construction. The red-brick Royal Pavilion Hotel next door would ultimately be engulfed.

Mediterranean manner', celebrating its centenary in 1966 with a complete re-fronting that removed all trace of the building's original Italianate design. Profits were ploughed back into the business to provide private bathrooms throughout and balconies to every sea-facing bedroom. Folkestone's once luxurious Royal Pavilion Hotel did not emerge well from wartime requisitioning and in 1955 was converted to a care home by Motyl Burstin, a Polish ex-seaman. He gradually restored parts of the Victorian building and demolished others until the surviving spaces could be encased in a huge new ship-shaped hotel with landmark raked-back upper floors. As work got underway in spring 1973 the thousand-room, £1 million project was christened Motel Burstin (opposite) by the town clerk and, for obvious reasons, the name stuck. Traditional seaside tourism could not have sustained such a venture into the 1980s but Folkestone's growth as a holiday port meant short-stay Continental package business kept the Motel Burstin afloat. That did not necessarily make it popular; a 1987 article prompted by its sale described it 'like the stern section of a stricken supertanker, high and dry, and on the rocks …'[44] Despite calls for its demolition the hotel is still operational today.

The Harbour

Burstin, Folkestone.

ET6057

The Dover Stage sought to offer
a new concept in hotel design
catering specifically to the coach trade.

Among the crop of brand new but often undistinguished
seaside hotels, two stand out for their innovative responses
to visitors arriving by road: the Dover 'coachotel' and the
Bournemouth 'Dekotel'. Hungarian-born architect Louis Erdi had
been commissioned by Graham Lyons to design Britain's first
American-style motel in 1954, and worked again for him on the
Dover Stage (opposite), a joint venture with Watney brewers
that was dubbed a 'coachotel' because of its specific mission to
cater for coach passengers. Opened in 1957, it was only the third
new hotel built since the war, managing in its design to straddle
Festival-style mixed materials with a fresh feel for massing. Instead
of facing the seafront on which it was built, the thin bedroom
block ran north–south, raised two storeys in the air on slim
V-shaped concrete piloti. Sea views came from oblique balconies
clad with cedar shingles. Prefabricated components reduced
costs, but a structural distinction was made with the low public
wing that housed ballroom and bars, which was built of timber
and brick. Although Dover had long been a seaside resort the
completion of a car ferry terminal with new drive-on-drive-off
facilities in 1953 hastened the growth of its modern port status

Bournemouth's Round House Hotel hid three levels of car parking behind the lattice-effect walls of its middle section.

and increased the need for hotel capacity to deal with coach passengers either side of their Channel crossing. In the late 1950s the Dover Stage lived up to its 'Ultra Modern' billing but with only 42 bedrooms it quickly became too small and was demolished in 1988. The patented Dekotel system proposed to meet the hotel shortage with modular concrete towers that integrated car parking into their structures. Only two were built; the first, at Bournemouth, designed by R Jelinek-Karl, was named for its unique shape. The Round House Hotel in the postcard opposite opened in 1969. Above its ground-floor bars and banqueting suite, a spiral ramp led to three floors of garaging hidden behind lattice-effect concrete panels, with 102 bedrooms on the upper levels away from the clamour of the street.

Towers had dual appeal for seaside developers. Not only did they translate the progressive spirit of inland housing estates to the coast, they were also crucial to the alluring image of foreign resorts Britons were fed in holiday brochures. Spain's lax planning regulations allowed unfettered growth along the beaches of the Costa del Sol; in the six years from 1959, Torremolinos alone saw the construction of 55 new hotels.

Of course, this transformation from virgin land to high-rise urban space was a world away from anything possible along Britain's already built-up seafronts, but that did not stop the imposition of often crassly intrusive blocks of flats. Even select Frinton-on-Sea was not immune. In the early 1960s its clifftop Greensward was insensitively pierced by the 12-storey Frinton Court, designed by Ronald Ward & Partners. In Margate, a renewed interest in brutalism has seen a recent turn of fortune for the 19-storey Arlington House (page 174) designed by Russell Diplock. A bold statement of intent, the tower formed part of a wider programme to create a new transport hub on what had been the old Margate Sands railway station; split-level parking could accommodate 400 cars and 100 coaches, with an additional coach station and taxi rank. A pedestrian shopping arcade offered a novel 'park and buy' experience. Above it, Arlington House was built from precast units on a reinforced concrete frame. The main elevations ran back from the sea but a cranked wave profile ensured all 142 flats enjoyed stunning views; continuous bands of aluminium glazing read as stripes across the white calcinated flint façades. Hopes embodied in 'build and they will come' luxury

The Clock Tower and Beach, Margate.

ET.4254

Opposite Arlington House by Russell Diplock was of a completely different scale to the rest of Margate Promenade.

Right The 1962 Bowling Lanes at Southend began a seaside trend for quirky roof shapes.

flats proved sadly misplaced. The development was unpopular and from its completion in 1963 occupancy levels remained stubbornly low and shops went untenanted. In 2011, plans to put a supermarket on the site were defeated by local campaigners, so maybe, with the right approach and an appreciation of the building's part in Margate's evolving story, Arlington House could yet fulfil its potential.

Private investment in resort entertainment remained strong through the 1960s and 70s as major national leisure operators built up their competing seaside portfolios. Between them Trust House Forte, Coral Leisure and the Rank Organisation bought up hotels, holiday camps and piers. Novelties shaping the sector included the latest American imports of bingo and ten-pin bowling, enthusiastically embraced by the over- and under-forties respectively. In 1962, Southend Pier (right) was something of a pioneer when its burned-down pavilion was replaced by a bowling centre, just two years after the mechanized game was introduced to the UK. Architects Silverton and Welton made a feature of the roof covering the play area with a grid of inverted pyramids on steel lattice girders; curtain walling on either side

Central Pier, Blackpool.

ET.5546

In 1966 Trust House Forte replaced the theatre on Blackpool Central Pier with an amusement arcade and cabaret bar.

of the lanes provided bowlers with natural light and expansive views. Amusement arcades proliferated around this time, too, as the permissive 1960 Gaming Act opened up the sector to multiple small operators. The massive expansion of coin-operated machines caused moral panic among sections of the community, and the government was forced to respond with the introduction of punitive taxes in 1968, a move which favoured big companies that could offset these extra costs with profits from the new cabaret show bars and discotheques that formed part of their self-styled leisure centres.

Trust House Forte acquired a group of piers which were revamped by Blackpool architects MacKeith Dickinson & Partners. The first to get a facelift from 1966 was Blackpool's Central Pier, where the promenade theatre gave way to a 'luxurious all-purpose family rendez-vous'.[45] The completed building housed the Golden Goose amusement arcade on its ground floor with a Dixieland Showbar on the storey above. The postcard opposite shows how colourful glass-reinforced plastic (GRP) and a roofline of architectural Toblerone helped disguise the basic steel shed construction. Quirky roof profiles became a trademark of the

The Pier, Southport

S.0557

The 1970 revamp of Southport Pier included the country's largest Dixieland Showbar to the right of the entrance and an unusually roofed Golden Fry restaurant to the left.

brand and the piers at Colwyn Bay and Llandudno got their share of pyramids after Trust House Forte took them over and added amusement arcades in 1968.

The interwar pavilion at Colwyn Bay survived but 1930s modernism was out of fashion, so the new owners proposed a refurbishment to make it 'more Victorian than the Victorians themselves would have achieved'. This was all the more bizarre when it transpired that the Victorian setting they aimed to recreate was that of a Mississippi paddle steamer from turn-of-the-century New Orleans. By 1970 Dixieland Showbars had moored at seven seaside resorts, including Morecambe, Rhyl, Great Yarmouth and Ramsgate. Staffed by waitresses in Charleston dresses and barmen wearing straw boaters, the largest of these cabaret venues was at Southport, where the Edwardian pier pavilion was demolished to make way for a giant wedge of a building. Here the fancy roof was reserved for the Golden Fry restaurant, seen to the left of the pier entrance in the postcard shown opposite; its 16 thick ridges rose to a central intersection with a silvery space-age quality. Skegness Pier tried to follow the mixed amusements and cabaret model after a group of local businessmen purchased it in 1966. Though the Sands Showbar was not a success, the pier entrance is now a rare survivor of the period, its gently sloping roof supported on exposed glulam beams over walls that feature tall windows and bright GRP panels.

Plastic fascias like those shown on page 180 gave seafront amusements an appropriately brash new look. Where arcades were in their highest concentration, along the Golden Miles of Blackpool and Great Yarmouth, competition generated design innovation. Until the late 1960s, the area south of Blackpool Tower retained its Victorian streetscape, with shops and arcades tacked onto ground-floor frontages. The era of large, purpose-built amusement sheds got underway with the 1968 Golden Mile Centre (page 181), funded by the Blackpool Tower Company, which had cash to invest following its acquisition by EMI. For the all-important promenade frontage Gordon Mackeith, resident architect to the Tower Company, commissioned an abstract mural from mosaic artist Jeanne Mount, which was inserted into the upper floor of boxy bow windows overhanging the multiple doors at street level. Inside, the arcade set a new industry standard with its fully carpeted ground floor; there were slot machines, a café and bingo with a full indoor funfair waiting at the top of the escalators.

New plastic materials were used to attract customers to
amusement arcades like this one at Ingoldmells near Skegness.

The 'Golden Mile' Beach and Tower, Blackpool.

ET.6165

Huge new amusement structures along Blackpool Promenade
included the Golden Mile Centre (second from right) and the
Penny Booth, later Funland (right).

It was not long before neighbouring sites spawned rival entertainment complexes. The 1976 Palatine Buildings was famous both for its eccentric roofline of stacked square openings and the Palace nightclub, which drew in clubbers from across the North West between 1986 and 2004. Next door, the Coral Leisure Group invested £4.5 million in its eponymous Coral Island (opposite), billed as the biggest leisure centre in the kingdom when it opened in 1978. Covering nearly two acres, it could hold 5,000 people with a bingo club for 1,500 and a glittering array of 400 amusement machines. The Penny Booth, subsequently renamed Funland, opened around the same time with a confident façade of three-dimensional forms. Its slim white pillars rising up through two floors to splayed triangular shapes could be a pop-art version of Denys Lasdun's 1963 Fitzwilliam College dining hall at Cambridge University. All these buildings had a flavour of the English Las Vegas about them, but with a visitor economy of £80 million based on more than 16 million holidays and day trips each year, Blackpool still had the power to present itself on its own terms. The smaller arcades along Great Yarmouth's Golden Mile were mostly add-ons to existing buildings so the appeal of neon signage, identified in the seminal 1972 book *Learning from Las Vegas* by Robert Venturi, Denise Scott Brown and Steve Izenour, had real commercial resonance. In the Golden Nugget, The Flamingo and The Mint (page 184), Norfolk's most popular resort adopted names and branding direct from the casinos of Fremont Street in Nevada's entertainment capital. Whether or not British tourists recognized the source, they certainly responded to the emphatic light displays.

At Blackpool Pleasure Beach, alterations continued to draw on exhibition precedents. Joseph Emberton remained in-house architect until his death in 1956, making postwar upgrades to the Ghost Train and Big Dipper. His successor was Jack Ratcliff of Howard V Lobb & Partners, former deputy director of architecture for the Festival of Britain and designer of the British Pavilion at the 1958 Brussels Expo. One of Ratcliff's first jobs was the Derby Racer, a traditional carousel ride with a twist. Its 56 horses raced underneath a polygonal dome of alloy steel with nine triangular sections of splayed windows. In 1966 a monorail was installed around the Pleasure Beach, bought from the World's Fair at Lausanne in Switzerland. Three years later the Astro Swirl

Great Yarmouth arcades borrowed their names
and light shows direct from Las Vegas.

The Pleasure Beach, BLACKPOOL.

ET.6026

New additions to Blackpool Pleasure Beach included the Astro
Swirl inside a Perspex dome, and the Space Tower.

The Isle of Man's newest attraction comprised two parts, the low white building of the Aquadrome and the Summerland solarium behind.

was unveiled, a brand-new cage ride based on the weightlessness machines used to train astronauts for the moon landings. To protect it from the marine environment Ratcliff designed the largest hemispherical dome outside America. Engineered in association with Ove Arup and Hawker Siddeley Aviation, it took 12 days to assemble the thousands of parts made from aluminium alloy extrusions and bronze-tinted Perspex. From 1975, visitors could travel to the top of the 48m (158ft)-high Space Tower in the postcard on page 185 to look down on the remodelled park.

Seaside attractions simply had to move on. This was especially true on the Isle of Man, which was competing for customers with Blackpool and could not fall back on the car day-trip market. In 1965 local architect James Philipps Lomas came up with an audacious scheme to create an artificial environment where the sun always shone, a space rather than a building, that would encapsulate everything the holidaymaker could want in a 'transparent seaside village'.[46] He worked up his plan with Brian Gelling, whose previous role at specialist leisure firm Gillinson, Barnett & Partners (GBP) helped secure their input as associate architects. A brutalist concrete swimming pool named the

Aquadrome opened first in 1969 under council auspices. However, it was the £1 million solarium and multi-tiered Summerland complex (opposite and page 188) that attracted international attention and a much-needed spike in visitor numbers. In its construction as much as its concept Summerland pushed to be a trend-setter. To the rear, the rocky cliff face was integrated into the structure, giving a genuine sense of bringing the outside in; photographs also call to mind the backdrop of a Bond villain's lair. In keeping with this cinematic space-age image, the promenade front and roof were clad in a new acrylic sheeting called Oroglas. By alternating the positions of the bronze-tinted pyramidal panels the architects created a unique faceted pattern across the façade. Warren Chalk's review in the *Architects' Journal* regretted that after all this the interior content did not sparkle with the pixie dust of 'Disney's twentieth century plastic fairy-tale land'; another commentator questioned where the original vision of an idealized Cornish or Mediterranean village had gone.[47] Commercial expedience dictated the mix of shows, arcade games, bars and crazy golf. Lessee Trust House Forte gave visitors the holiday diversions they were used to and in that there was a sort

Summerland, Douglas, Isle of Man.

51

SUMMERLAND. DOUGLAS, I. O. M.

Summerland promised an artificial seaside
where the sun always shone.

of back-handed compliment to the traditional British seaside.
Chalk cautiously judged that Summerland might just be the
beginning of a reinvigoration of the nation's coastal resorts, but it
was not to be. On 2 August 1973, barely two years after opening,
a terrible fire raged through Summerland killing 50 people. An
inquiry found inadequate means of escape, due to the operational
division of the solarium and swimming pool, as well as an unsafe
level of combustibility in the Oroglas, which should never have
been used in such quantity in such a setting. Summerland was
rebuilt as a low white box. The sports centre which rose from
the ashes was understandably focused on safe functionalism but
the hope it would save the Isle of Man's holiday industry was long
extinguished by the time of reopening in 1978.

That Summerland proved to be a false start does not mean
it was the end of attempts to revive the seaside offer. From the
mid-1960s municipal solutions varied according to community need
because the cost of indoor pool and sports venues necessitated

year-round operation. The 1965 Afan Lido next to Aberavon Beach was a trailblazer, the first purpose-built sports centre in Wales, incorporating a competition-size swimming pool, gym, spa and sports hall suitable for concert use. It aimed to boost tourism at the same time as catering for the steelworkers of Port Talbot.

Worthing's 1968 Aquarena was one of the first to adopt a brand name. Though swimmers welcomed the long-awaited pool, the building by Derek Walker, John Attenborough and Bryn Jones was widely despised as a brutal affront to the terraced boarding houses and promenade gardens surrounding it. Claims that the exterior of brick, concrete, aluminium and zinc would be virtually maintenance-free were undermined when structural faults required the pool to be practically rebuilt from 1977. Torquay's Edwardian Marine Spa pool was nearing the end of its useful life when the council briefed architectural firm Sir Basil Spence, Bonnington & Collins in 1967. Their scheme was to incorporate indoor and outdoor pools, cafeterias, car parking and a multi-purpose entertainment hall in a radical series of floating terraces overlooking Beacon Cove. National economic woes saw the plan dropped, though a version of it was built in the early 1970s by borough architect Ray Banks. Sun terraces around a small outdoor pool were based on a hexagonal grid, while the building itself was defined by open concrete arches that referenced the round-headed windows of the demolished spa building. The council promised facilities for tourists *and* locals but then put operation of the centre out to tender just weeks before its completion. Coral Leisure won the contract and when the Devonian Coral Island (page 190) opened in June 1977 its nightclub, restaurants, prize bingo and fruit machines were aimed squarely at holidaymakers. Residents' discontent grew when Coral announced winter closing after the first season. Routine maintenance was not undertaken and within a decade this strikingly original seaside building was condemned to dereliction.

'CORAL ISLAND', TORQUAY   C37

Torquay's attempt at modern Riviera glamour paired concrete
arches with hexagonal decks around a swimming pool.

OASIS POOL, HUNSTANTON

The Oasis fun pool at Hunstanton opened in 1987
with a self-supporting reinforced plastic roof.

RHYL SUN CENTRE

Rhyl Sun Centre aimed to be a one-stop seaside destination with varied water and entertainment experiences including a surf pool (top right) and remote-controlled car racing (bottom left).

Decisive change came with the adoption of freeform pools that prioritized family water fun over swimming. While Summerland was under construction, GBP worked with Whitley Bay council on proposals for a (250ft) 76m-high translucent pyramid made up of staggered terraces. Billed as a closed-in 'Riviera resort' the £2 million seafront solarium was based around a 'lake-type swimming pool surrounded by tropical plants', with an exhibition hall, nightclub, teenage discotheque and restaurants.[48] Despite strong public support for an amenity designed to put the North East's favourite resort back on the map, opposition from a small but vociferous group of residents led to a public inquiry that ruled against the plans in October 1969. GBP were retained to deliver a much-reduced £500,000 building which, when it opened in April 1974, was still only the third leisure pool in the country, narrowly pipped by Bletchley and Rotherham.

On the Norfolk coast Hunstanton Urban District Council also tried to take the initiative, sending a delegation to the Isle of Man, then commissioning Lomas and GBP to design an indoor entertainment centre for a site next to their pier. The model produced in summer 1970 was based around two geodesic domes, the largest of which would house a 33m (108ft)-diameter lagoon with water slide. When private development finance failed to materialize the plans were dropped, but the town's open-air swimming pool had already been demolished; it would be 17 years before the Oasis leisure centre replaced it. The postcard on page 191 shows the self-supporting reinforced plastic roof designed by West Norfolk Council architects to cover the new indoor fun pool.

It was in Rhyl's 1980 Sun Centre (opposite) that GBP finally got to fulfil their vision for an enclosed resort. Brochures urged potential visitors to sample the 'Great Indoors' of 'warm air, warm water [and] real waves lapping against a gently sloping beach fringed with palm trees and exotic sub-tropical flora'.[49] The centre's roof-top monorail was reputedly a world first and no other European country could yet boast an indoor surf pool like Rhyl's. To keep visitors occupied by the blue waters of the Tropical Lagoon there was a Sunset restaurant, suntan beds and a Tropical Island entertainments area; children had their own splash pool, radio-controlled racing-car circuit and character slides Pink Elephant and Friendly Octopus. Everything was accommodated within what *Building* magazine called a 'Fosteresque' shed. The

The exterior of Rhyl's Sun Centre did little to reference its seafront location because this was becoming increasingly irrelevant.

architects themselves rather wistfully described it as 'the twentieth century answer to the seaside pier' but, as reviewers noted, 'the only reference to the North Wales seaside by which the centre is actually located is the view through the glazed walls'.[50] The postcard opposite shows an industrial-looking structure of corrugated aluminium and bronze-tinted PVC. The lack of seaside reference points was a sign of things to come, but it was a major achievement just getting it finished: industrial disputes, inflation and design changes caused a two-year overrun and a £2.25 million overspend. The Sun Centre did better in its first season than expected but it was becoming harder for councils to build new attractions. That they kept trying must be to their credit.

At Morecambe, the need for expensive structural repairs to the underused Super Swimming Stadium prompted the appointment of Newcastle-based architects Faulkner-Brown, Hendy, Watkinson, Stonor, the firm responsible for the seminal Bletchley Pyramid leisure centre near Milton Keynes. Despite representations to save the lido, demolition was approved in April 1976 and construction began on an outdoor heated pool surrounded by sunbathing lawns. Circular changing facilities for

a thousand people were built under an attention-grabbing roof of flamboyant scalloped profile. Holidaymakers surveyed on opening day in June 1979 'were pleased with it, some even comparing it with places in Spain and Hawaii'.[51] Locals complained that the pool was too small but the original project suffered grievous financial cutbacks and the council was lucky to secure a third of the costs from EEC regional development funding, the only tourist facility granted such an allocation. Phase two was a £900,000 Superdome for summer entertainments and winter sports use. Unfortunately, its Perspex roof caused the hall to overheat and mitigating treatment compromised its design quality.

Another specialist leisure firm was the Bridgend-based Module 2. Their 1981 Marina Centre replaced Great Yarmouth's interwar bathing pool and Marina band enclosure with a huge sports, entertainment and conference venue, centred around a Continental-sounding 'Piazza'. The leisure pool and indoor beach were 'designed to create a warm Mediterranean atmosphere for the whole family to enjoy'.[52] As elsewhere, there was little reference to the sands outside, though the roof of aquamarine pyramids did contribute to a modern seaside vernacular. Cleethorpes leisure

The Leisure Centre, Cleethorpes.

ET.6522

Cleethorpes Leisure Centre was designed
to form part of the town's sea defences
with views across the Humber Estuary
from its free-form leisure pool.

pool (opposite) featured the trademark Module 2 interior of
tiled walls in shades of brown, red and white, along with the now
obligatory (but functionally useless) indoor parasols. Exterior
plastic panels suggested large switches suited to the dawning
computer age, while the deep eaves of the overhanging roof gave
the building a kind of gravitas. Dubbed 'The jewel of the resort',
it was completed in 1982 ahead of schedule and on budget.[53]

Seaside resorts embraced leisure centres in the whole-
hearted way they had once embraced open-air lidos, and new
space-frame technology helped meet demand. Using truss-like
structures made of tubular steel interconnected in geometric
patterns, buildings could be simultaneously strong and lightweight.
Brighton's 1981 Prince Regent swimming pool was the first in
the country to employ a space structure, engineered by Ronald
G Taylor & Associates. This cleared a path for mixed-use leisure
centres in unconventional shapes. Blackpool Borough Council
sacrificed its 1923 Open Air Baths for an equally massive
statement building, named for its 14m (46ft)-high sloping walls
meant to look like a giant sandcastle, a rare reference to the
context of its location. Opened in 1986, with four swimming

pools, cafés and shops, Blackpool Sandcastle is still the UK's
largest indoor water park. The 1988 Southsea Pyramids was
named for the three pyramid roofs built over a central leisure
pool and flanking structures containing a piazza and winter
garden. Both centres were designed by Charles Smith Architects,
also responsible for Bridlington Leisure World and Eastbourne
Sovereign Centre.

Whether based on water attractions or the flashing
lights of arcades and discos, the evolution of artificial seaside
spaces was a direct response to the rising expectations of British
holidaymakers. Package deals made the transition to foreign
promenades an easy one, with the consequence that traditional
resorts began to lose faith in their core attractions. By the closing
decades of the 20th century the British seaside had a serious
image problem.

5

DECLINE AND NEW HOPE

THE BRIGHTON CENTRE

BRIGHTON

Previous page The Sea Life Centre at Southend was one of many built at resorts in the 1980s and 90s. **Above** In 1977 the pointed roofscape of Russell Diplock's Top Rank Suite, now Odeon, was joined by the heavy presence of the Brighton Centre by the same practice.

I n 1980, the West Sussex seaside got a new combined theatre, café, bar and multi-purpose hall in the Bognor Regis Centre, designed by London architects Farrington Dennys Fisher. It was the showpiece of a £1.5 million redevelopment of the Esplanade and yet it turned its back on that essential seafront space. The *Architects' Journal* complimented the building's design and value for money but could not reconcile it with its location: 'it owes more … to a community centre in some provincial town than to the effervescent wit and vulgarity of traditional seaside architecture.'[54] It was an observation that could be applied more widely to structures erected by the sea from the late 1970s onwards, as resorts increasingly showed disdain for the very things that made them distinctive.

In large part this was due to falling visitor demand. Domestic tourism hit its peak in 1972–3 then fell into a period of depression after the first international oil crisis. In the decade to 1985 main holidays taken in Britain fell from 27 to 20 million, while the number of overseas holidays leapt up from 12 to 22 million.[55] This seismic shift in favour of foreign destinations continued for the rest of the century as the costs of flying were dramatically reduced and credit cards removed the need to save up for more expensive holiday options; people could have their fun in the sun and pay for it later. The example of Morecambe shows how dramatic the collapse could be. In 1973

the value of tourism in the resort was put at £46.6 million; by 1990 it had dropped to a mere £6.5 million.[56] On top of this, the political climate, which had been favourable since the 1920s, now conspired against resorts. The autonomy to pursue ambitious municipal attractions was curtailed after the 1974 local government reorganization, which subsumed seaside councils into larger areas with conflicting inland priorities. The gradual loss of in-house engineering and architecture departments, as well as the introduction of compulsory competitive tendering by the 1988 Local Government Act, made direct involvement in provision of tourism facilities harder still.

Some of the biggest English resorts tried to refocus their efforts on the conference trade, which had provided important income for decades but now seemed to offer a route to economic salvation. Investment in huge new facilities was only viable for places with sufficient high-quality hotel accommodation, and those were few. In September 1977, Prime Minister James Callaghan opened the Brighton Centre (opposite), designed by Russell Diplock Associates as the final element in the Churchill Square development. A brutalist edifice of textured concrete and brick, it cost £9 million and did the job required of it; by 1988 it had brought an estimated 350,000 delegates and visitors to the town, injecting £53 million and stimulating hotel improvements. Hoping to repeat this success, the looming brick bulk of

Bournemouth International Centre may be a popular venue but it is a lumpen presence above the West Beach.

Bournemouth International Centre (opposite) opened in 1984, almost 20 years after it was first proposed. Since extended, the original design by Module 2 featured two large halls, a leisure pool and trendy wine bar. Module 2 was also the main contractor for Torquay's 1987 English Riviera Centre (page 204), which likewise offered a vast conference arena, exhibition space and leisure pool with additional health and fitness facilities. Two hotels had to be compulsorily purchased and demolished to secure its prime site, but rising costs and poor returns made it a contentious addition to the seafront. The buildings at Brighton, Bournemouth and Torquay were necessary at the time but they were not pretty and they were not good seaside.

A more common situation around the coast was for demolition of older attractions without any plan for their replacement. This loss of key structures contributed to the hollowing out of seaside identity. Among the buildings discussed in this book, Lee-on-the-Solent pier was demolished in 1971, Aberystwyth King's Hall in 1989, Gourock's Cragburn Pavilion and Ventnor Royal Victoria Pier in 1993. Lidos were lost at Ramsgate in 1975, Portobello in 1988, New Brighton in 1990 and Hastings in 1993.

Bournem

ational Centre

ENGLISH RIVIERA CENTRE & GARDENS, TORQUAY C71

Torquay's English Riviera Centre opened for sports,
conferences and exhibitions in 1987.

The Three Shells, Western Esplanade, Southend-on-Sea   S.0458

The Three Shells café at Southend revived
the idea of seaside playfulness in 1983.

LOWESTOFT

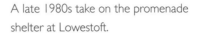

A late 1980s take on the promenade
shelter at Lowestoft.

However, it was not all gloom. Glimpses of seaside
playfulness were still visible, for example in the roof that gave its
name to the Three Shells café at Southend, photographed soon
after its 1983 opening in the postcard on page 205. At South
Shields, the metal railings of the 1988 raised promenade were well
handled and the sheltered space underneath is genuinely beautiful
with its tiled floor patterns and relief shell motifs on the ceiling
designed by Bryan Blake. At Lowestoft, bright red lamp standards
and mushroom shelters (opposite) updated the Esplanade in the
late 1980s. The spread of Sea Life Centres around British resorts
was also an important success story. The first site was created in
1979 at Oban, on Scotland's west coast, and by 1996 there were
15 coastal centres with innovative underwater tunnels that gave
visitors the sensation of walking along the seabed. At Blackpool,
Europe's largest display of tropical sharks moved into the Golden
Mile Centre in 1990; Scarborough Sea Life Centre (page 208)
opened in an eye-catching building of white pyramids in 1991 and
the Weston-super-Mare centre was built on a brand-new 84m
(275ft)-long pier over the beach in 1995. The big blue gables of
Rhyl's 1992 Sea Life Centre were part of a major promenade

Scarborough Sea Life Centre opened in purpose-built
pyramids beside the North Bay in 1991.

Rhyl Children's Village was a colourful if unsuccessful
attempt to reinvigorate the seafront.

The simple cone profiles of Ilfracombe's
Landmark Theatre contrast with the general
Victoriana of the North Devon resort.

redevelopment that included a 500-space underground car park,
open events arena and the Children's Village (page 209) designed
by Forrec in a colourful Disney-cum-shopping mall style.

More significant was the 1998 completion of a new seaside
theatre at Ilfracombe (opposite) in North Devon. Architect Tim
Ronalds produced a design to meet the challenges of rough
weather blowing in from the Bristol Channel that was also
aesthetically pleasing from all angles. His appropriately named
Landmark Theatre is defined by two striking white cones, each
built using a double layer of brick that required the expertise of
specialist bricklayers. Known locally as Madonna's Bra, the theatre
had its detractors, but the North Devon Journal praised it for daring
to be different: 'At long last this is an opportunity for the town
to forge ahead and reinvent the popularity that it enjoyed in the
Victorian era.'[57]

As the end of the 20th century approached there were
signs of a growing interest in the heritage of seaside architecture.
The pastiche Victorian used at Eastbourne Pier in 1991, to replace
the streamlined entrance building of 40 years earlier, and the
uPVC winter garden-style East Point Pavilion of 1992 at Lowestoft,

ILFRACOMBE

Tate St Ives borrowed from the 1930s
seaside aesthetic and began a wave of
art galleries at the coast.

recognized 19th-century precedents in a way that represented
a form of progress after so many Victorian seaside buildings had
been demolished. In 1986 the De La Warr Pavilion was made a
Grade I listed building. It had suffered considerable degradation to
its fabric and status over the preceding decade so its inclusion in
the nation's top 2.5 per cent of historic structures was a turning
point. The Pavilion Trust was formed in 1989 and full restoration
was finally completed in 2005. Evidence of the De La Warr's
continuing influence was clear to see in the beachfront elevation
of Tate St Ives (opposite), by Eldred Evans and David Shalev. This
building was important for its choice of design inspiration but
also for its new perspective on seaside visitor attractions. Since
it opened in 1993, seafront public sculpture and modern art
galleries have multiplied around the coast, with hugely beneficial
effect. Another notable trend was the gentrification of smaller
seaside towns. Media reports of rising beach-hut prices from the
mid-1990s suggested the quiet rediscovery of traditional seaside
pleasures by the very middle-class people who had rejected them
for foreign adventures earlier in the century. Sleepy Southwold
(page 214) in Suffolk became a surprising new Mecca, its idyllic

In the late 1990s Southwold became
famous for its expensive beach huts, and
the buildings on its new pier maintained
a similar sense of scale.

beach huts appearing in national tourism marketing material. This
renaissance was aided by the dream of businessman Christopher
Iredale to see Southwold Pier rebuilt; having purchased what little
was left of it in 1987 he and his wife overhauled the entrance
pavilion then, in July 2001, opened the first new pier to be built in
Britain since the 1950s.

The most successful seaside resorts of the past were
the ones hardest hit by the decline in domestic tourism.
Demographically speaking, it was a case of people with money
going elsewhere, which left resorts like Blackpool, Great
Yarmouth and Margate to cater for those on limited budgets.
Without a mixed economy of visitors it was hard to make the
necessary investment to attract new audiences back. That is now
changing. Since the Millennium there have been exciting new
architecture and heritage-led projects by the sea. Hopefully the
best of our surviving 20th-century seaside buildings can be part of
that progress into the future.

THREATS AND RESTORATION

by CATHERINE CROFT

D espite their innovation, delight and grip on the popular imagination, seaside buildings have had a tough time, and continue to do so. The specific economic ups and (mainly) downs of the British seaside in the later part of the 20th century have inevitably affected investment in their maintenance. Something as simple as a blocked gutter can rapidly lead to leaks, and for many buildings, their exposed locations and the prevalence of stormy seaside weather means that without constant vigilance and keeping on top of damage, a downhill spiral can be rapid and hard to reverse.

Many significant 20th-century buildings throughout the UK have inevitably suffered neglect, especially in the period when their innovative character has fallen out of fashion, and the cycle of taste has yet to recognize their latent potential. But it's the combination of seaside economics and a harsh seaside climate that has been especially challenging for many of the buildings celebrated in this book.

For concrete buildings there's another specific seaside issue: salt. Salt is sodium chloride, and chlorides and concrete are a disastrous combination. Nothing speeds up the decay of concrete and causes its smooth, sharply faceted façades to blister and spall faster than salt. And it's that crispness and preciseness that makes such a big contribution to many of the buildings in this book, especially the Modern Movement and art deco ones. Salt destroys the natural alkalinity of concrete, and this means that the steel reinforcement within it is no longer protected from corrosion. Rusty concrete expands enormously, exploding the concrete surface. Exposed rusty rebar looks dreadful, and epitomizes neglect and decay – and the sense of depression is exacerbated by netting or boards to catch lumps of spalling concrete. Salt gets into seaside concrete in a variety of ways, sometimes at the point of construction, when the proximity of beach sand or pebbles makes their inclusion in the concrete mix supremely tempting – which is fine as long as they are thoroughly rinsed to get rid of all the salt, but this was not always done. In addition, throughout the life of a building, the impact of wind-driven salt spray takes a toll – an impact I was all too well aware of earlier this year at Embassy Court, the 11-storey block of flats on the Brighton seafront designed by Wells Coates and completed in 1935, when I sat with

The Midland Hotel, Morecambe, in a
state of dilapidation before renovation.

residents as visibility reduced to almost zero and rain lashed at us. In that case the metal window frames are especially vulnerable too, and the challenge of caring for the building was brought vividly home to me.

Part of the sense of wonder and awe many of the structures in this book evoke is down to their sheer size: making them testament to a different world, when extraordinary numbers of seaside visitors far exceeded those we see today. There is still demand for 11-storey blocks of flats with fabulous views, but not for huge cinemas and theatres, nor for some of the pools and promenades. Those massive crowds of mid-century visitors feel like a different, hardier species, happy to swim and sunbathe regardless of the chilly temperatures we can all too easily imagine, despite the optimistic sunshine of alluring posters. Finding new uses for mammoth buildings is always harder and more expensive than repurposing more modest ones.

However there have been some amazing and inspirational conservation success stories. Mendelsohn and Chermayeff's De La Warr Pavilion, Bexhill-on-Sea, opened to the public for the first time on 12 December 1935. Seventy years on, *The Guardian* used

the classic accolade 'restored to its former glory' to headline its article marking the building's reopening as a centre for contemporary arts in October 2005. The Pavilion had narrowly avoided being sold off by a despairing Rother District Council (there were plans to convert it to a Wetherspoons pub), but a scheme by John McAslan and Partners, with Heritage Lottery funding and a huge amount of local support, came to its rescue. I love its defiant slogan, 'Est. 1935. Modern Ever Since', but there were undoubtedly times when being modern was not something that acted in its favour. That restoration itself is now 20 years old, and another round of investment is needed. Despite its Grade II* status, initial 21st-century proposals included a massive extension which C20 Society felt would be very damaging, but we are now optimistic that a more sympathetic scheme will be forthcoming.

Oliver Hill's Midland Hotel, Morecambe Bay, built in 1933, was also once supremely glamorous, but had fallen into what developer Tom Bloxham of Urban Splash lamented as a 'sad decline' before his firm took it on and restored it with architects Union North and Avanti, reopening it, complete with seahorse sculptures, in 2013. The project was a great success, and as

The Turner Contemporary gallery, opened
in 2011 on the seafront at Margate.

Bloxham notes, its impact was more than local: 'the hotel was a
symbol of renaissance for Morecambe but as a seaside icon tens
of thousands of people were genuinely attached to it.'

Other notable restorations have included Saltdean Lido
and the Jubilee Pool at Penzance. In both cases, adding ground-
source heat pumps means that the water is now warmer and
swimming over a longer season is viable. Currently underway is the
restoration of the Rothesay Pavilion, on the Isle of Bute. Designed
by James Carrick and built in 1938, it aims to become 'a social hub
and economic multiplier for the community' as well as a tourist
attraction, very much developing a broader remit which seems
increasingly necessary and compelling.

There is good news, too, as far as the potential recognition
of very late 20th century and 21st century heritage goes – there
are plenty of notable recent commissions which will surely qualify
for listing in the not-too-distant future. Kathryn Ferry includes
Tim Ronald's Landmark Theatre at Ilfracombe, and more recently
there has been an astonishing clutch of seaside art galleries. The
Turner Contemporary opened its doors in Margate in 2011,
built on the prominent site of the boarding house where

J M W Turner stayed during his visits to the town. Chipperfield Architects' design clusters six two-storey crystalline volumes, with mono-pitched roofs, close to the shore, and visible right across the bay as soon as visitors exit the railway station. Shortly after, Hastings Contemporary (originally named the Jerwood Gallery) opened in 2012 to house the Jerwood Foundation's collection of modern British paintings and drawings, as well as temporary exhibitions. It won a RIBA National Award and a Civic Trust Award, and was included in *The Observer*'s list of the top buildings of 2012. Praising it at the time in *The Sunday Times*, Hugh Pearman, now Chair of C20 Society, described it as 'A little jewel of a gallery, beautifully considered and detailed'. It is by HAT Projects, and its dark ceramic cladding references the adjacent huts used for drying fishing nets. Along the south coast at Littlehampton, in 2008, the East Beach Café was the first real building completed by Thomas Heatherwick, who wanted to create a space that would be both 'a prospect and refuge', a place to look out to sea and feel safe and sheltered. It was commissioned by Jane Wood and Sophie Murray, who then picked Asif Khan (straight out of the Architectural Association School of Architecture) for their smaller West Beach Café, a structure made from galvanized steel

and oversized sash windows that opens up in glorious weather, hunkering down when it's bad.

But as well as prompting me to review the conservation issues, past, present and future, for the British seaside, I am struck by how vividly the previous chapters in this book not only celebrate the incredibly ambitious and the most modest of projects, but also vividly convey the impact of the British seaside on the lives of British people, and the changing way we relax, have fun and take our holidays. The story Kathryn Ferry tells chimes with personal and family histories for almost all of us living in the UK today, and prompts us to recall enjoyable times and positive experiences, sunlit days captured in photo albums and anecdotes that have become the stuff of family legend. Although top of the list in our family is the time I got locked in a public lavatory on the seafront at Budleigh Salterton, for instance, and my mother had to beg a penny from a passer-by to release me. (Was that positive or traumatic? I think I can remember the sense of claustrophobia as an early special experience!)

My grandparents' only holidays were single, annual weeks by the seaside. One set were West Yorkshire mill workers, who set off by train when the factories closed down. Each week had a distinctive name, with the Brighouse Rush followed by Bradford's Bolling Tide. They would head out sometimes for the Lancashire west coast (Morecambe or Blackpool), sometimes east to Scarborough, still in Yorkshire but definitely not home turf, and part of the ritual was watching the previous week's holidaymakers heading homewards. They stayed in boarding houses where you had to take your own food, but the landlady cooked it for you (which seems a very strange and unsatisfactory arrangement). Activities included meeting up with relatives, sitting in beach huts, and not much more. Neither could swim, and even paddling seems to have been a bit daunting. It all sounds rather drab, but was definitely seen as aspirational, progressive and a highlight of the year. My paternal grandparents were Londoners, so for them it was Worthing and maybe a bit more sunshine, a little less windswept and more participation in the entertainments on offer.

My parents, before I was born, drove with friends who had a car across what they called 'the Continent' as far as what was then Yugoslavia, majoring on cities rather than seeking out foreign coasts. But when my sister and came along, it was the British seaside again, but less a resort-based holiday and more striving to locate a real place, with a bit of older history. After one trip to Dorset and the Budleigh Salterton experience, they got a car themselves and tried something different. St David's, in Pembrokeshire, has a long sandy beach, but it turns its back on the sea, and it's dominated by the Cathedral and Bishop's Palace. Moreover, mainly we headed out of town to tiny coves, ideally with no infrastructure, parking on the verge of narrow sunken lanes, taking a picnic with us, and looking for rock pools and birdwatching. Soon after that it was rental cottages, Pembrokeshire again and then the Scottish West Coast, before the discovery of French gîtes drew us across the channel again, and inland in search of vineyards, wine-tasting and more hikes and medieval architecture.

Since having a daughter myself, I've developed a taste for cold-water swimming, and I'm spending more time at the traditional British seaside I largely missed out on as a child. As climate change and a growing awareness of the impact of global tourism make us ever more aware of our need to consider the impact we have on the world, particularly through travel and leisure, perhaps the time is right for more holidays here at home: donkey rides might not be good for donkeys, and seaside rock might not be great for our teeth or our waistlines, but British seaside architecture is uplifting, diverse and certainly rich in stories.

NOTES

1 | INTERWAR CLASSICAL

[1] *Swanage Times and Directory*, 12 February 1927, p. 5; 31 August 1928, p. 5

[2] *East Kent Times and Mail*, 11 October 1922, p. 8; 21 July 1926, p. 5

[3] 'A "Roman" Bath', *Fleetwood Chronicle*, 9 June 1916, p. 2

[4] 'A New Colosseum', *Lancashire Evening Post*, 4 June 1923, p. 2

[5] Allan Brodie and Matthew Whitfield, *Blackpool's Seaside Heritage*, English Heritage: 2014, p. 97

[6] 'Seaside Architecture: Great Yarmouth and Blackpool', *Official Architect*, October 1937, p. 46

[7] 'Wonderful Developments at Skegness', *Boston Guardian*, 28 May 1927, p. 4

[8] Cited in 'Beauty of the Pavilion', *Worthing Herald*, 23 October 1926, p. 10

[9] 'The New Pier Pavilion', *Worthing Gazette*, 30 June 1926, p. 6

[10] 'New Pier Pavilion', *Worthing Herald*, 26 June, 1926, p. 1

[11] Julian Holder and Elizabeth McKellar (eds), *Neo-Georgian Architecture 1880–1970: a reappraisal*, Historic England: 2016, p. 17

[12] 'Souvenir of the Opening of the Winter Gardens Pavilion, Weston-super-Mare, July 14 1927,' p. 2

[13] 'Royal Visit to Folkestone', *Folkestone, Hythe, Sandgate and Cheriton Herald*, 16 July 1927, p. 2

[14] 'Making Modern Brighton', *Daily News*, 26 April 1928, p. 5

[15] M L Anderson, 'The New Pavilion at Hastings', *Architects' Journal*, 20 April 1927, pp. 549–50

2 | DECO, MODERN, MODERNE

[16] Ferdinand Tuohy, 'The New Bronze Age', *The Graphic*, 23 August 1930, p. 298

[17] 'On Going to the Seaside', *Official Architect*, September 1937, p. 9

[18] 'The New Pier Pavilion, Colwyn Bay', *The Architect and Building News*, 1 June 1934, www.victoriapier.co.uk/pavilion.php

[19] *Worthing Gazette*, 24 July 1935, p. 9; for photograph see 1 August 1935, p. 1

[20] Peter Maitland, 'The Architect', *Architectural Review*, July 1936, p. 26

[21] Charles McKean, *The Scottish Thirties*, Rutland Press: 1987, p. 93

[22] 'Scotland Takes the Plunge: A Wet Boom', *Reynold's Illustrated News*, 16 August 1931, p. 7

[23] 'Palace Court Hotel, Bournemouth', *The Architect and Building News*, 10 January 1936, pp. 65–8

[24] '£30,000 Holiday Camp as New Skegness Garden Suburb', *Skegness News*, 28 August 1935, p. 1; 1936.

3 | FESTIVAL STYLE AT THE SEASIDE

[25] *Illustrated London News*, 26 May 1951, p. 851

[26] Mary Banham and Bevis Hillier (eds), *A Tonic to the Nation: The Festival of Britain 1951*, Thames & Hudson: 1976, pp. 53–4

[27] 'New Pier Entrance an "Artistic job"', *Eastbourne Herald*, 17 March 1951, p. 14

[28] Hannen Swaffer in the *Daily Herald*: on Blackpool, 2 August 1952, p. 6; Brighton, 5 August 1952, p. 4; Margate, 6 August 1952 p. 4; Scarborough, 7 August 1952, p. 4

[29] Alistair Fair, *Modern Playhouses: An Architectural History of Britain's New Theatres, 1945–1985*, Oxford University Press: 2018, p. 17; John K. Walton, *The British Seaside: Holidays and resorts in the twentieth century*, Manchester University Press: 2000, p. 63

[30] 'Boscombe Pier repair now permitted', *Bournemouth Echo*, 5 January 1955 (press cuttings in Bournemouth Library)

31 Elain Harwood, *Mid-Century Britain; Modern Architecture 1938–1963*, Batsford: 2021, p. 222

32 Supplement to the *Portsmouth Evening News*, 1 June 1961, pp. 29–36

33 Harwood, op. cit., p. 256

34 'Dunoon's New Pavilion Opened', *The Scotsman*, 26 April 1958, p. 6

35 Cited in Fair, op. cit. p. 61; 'The Congress, Eastbourne', *The Stage*, 13 June 1963, p. 15

36 John Robinson, 'Torquay Today – New Amenities', in special supplement to the *Municipal Review*, December 1961, pp. 1, 4

37 'Architect praises "Adventure Spirit"', *Torbay Express and South Devon Echo*, 3 April 1957, p. 5

38 'The Floral Hall', *Liverpool Daily Post* (Welsh edition), 31 March 1959, p. 2

39 'Festival Pavilion at Skegness', *Official Architecture and Planning*, Vol. 27, No. 4, April 1964, p. 415

4 | THE BRITISH COSTAS

40 Fair, op. cit.; Otto Saumarez-Smith, 'The Lost World of the British Leisure Centre', *History Workshop Journal*, 2019

41 Cited in Walton, op. cit., p. 63; and Nigel J. Morgan and Annette Pritchard, *Power and Politics at the Seaside: The Development of Devon's Resorts in the Twentieth Century*, University of Exeter Press: 1999, p. 39

42 Morgan and Pritchard, op. cit., p. 40

43 Clifford Musgrave, *Life in Brighton from the earliest times to the present*, Faber and Faber: 1970, pp. 449–51

44 'What now for Motel Burstin?' *The Folkestone, Hythe, Sandgate and Cheriton Herald*, 28 August 1987, p. 22

45 'Central Pier's Face-lift … Forte's big plans for Blackpool', *The Stage*, 12 June 1967, p. 3

46 Ian Phillips, 'Summerland Fire Disaster', available at www.summerlandfiredisaster.co.uk, p. 157

47 Warren Chalk, 'Summerland: Appraisal', *Architects' Journal*, 22 September 1971, p. 638

48 'North may get £2 million "Riviera Resort"', *Newcastle Journal*, 27 September 1968, p. 8

49 'Rhyl's Tropical Island', advertising brochure

50 'South Sea Environment in North Wales', *Building*, 18 July 1980, p. 116; 'Beside the Seaside', *Architects' Journal*, 16 July 1980, p. 122

51 'We've got a ticket to ride – into the 1980s', *Morecambe Visitor*, 26 June 1979 (press cuttings in Morecambe Library)

52 'Marina Centre – Opens Summer '81', promotional brochure

53 'All set to open', *Grimsby Daily Telegraph*, 2 December 1982, p. 7

5 | DECLINE AND NEW HOPE

54 Charles Knevitt, 'Beside the Seaside: Bognor Regis Leisure Centre', *Architects' Journal*, 3 September 1980, p. 446

55 Morgan and Pritchard, op. cit., p. 42

56 Association of District Councils, 1993, cited in Tim Gale, 'Late Twentieth Century Cultural Change and the Decline and Attempted Rejuvenations of the British Seaside Resort as a Long Holiday Destination: A Case Study of Rhyl, North Wales', unpublished PhD thesis, University of Wales, 2001, p. 30

57 'Theatre of the highest quality will benefit the whole region', *North Devon Journal; Landmark Theatre Supplement*, 30 April 1998, p. viii

FURTHER READING

Banham, Mary and Hillier, Bevis eds., *A Tonic to the Nation: The Festival of Britain 1951* (Thames and Hudson, 1976)

Brodie, Allan, *The Seafront* (Historic England, 2018)

Brodie, Allan and Whitfield, Matthew, *Blackpool's Seaside Heritage* (English Heritage, 2014)

Croll, Andy, *Barry Island: The Making of a Seaside Playground c. 1790–c. 1965* (University of Wales Press, 2020)

Easdown, Martin, *Lancashire's Seaside Piers* (Wharncliffe Books, 2009)

Fair, Alistair, *Modern Playhouses: An Architectural History of Britain's New Theatres, 1945–1985* (Oxford University Press, 2018)

Fairley, Alistair, *De La Warr Pavilion: The Modernist Masterpiece* (Merrell, 2006)

Ferry, Kathryn, *Seaside 100: A History of the British Seaside in 100 Objects* (Unicorn, 2020)

Beach Huts and Bathing Machines (Shire, 2009)

Franklin, Geraint with Nick Dermott and Allan Brodie, *Ramsgate: The Town and its Seaside Heritage* (Historic England, 2020)

Gordon, Ian and Inglis, Simon, *Great Lengths: The Historic Indoor Swimming Pools of Britain* (English Heritage, 2009)

Gray, Fred, *The Architecture of British Seaside Piers* (The Crowood Press, 2020)

Designing the Seaside: Architecture, Society and Nature (Reaktion Books, 2006)

Harwood, Elain, *Brutalist Britain: Buildings of the 1960s and 70s* (Batsford, 2022)

Mid-Century Britain: Modern Architecture 1938–1963 (Batsford, 2021)

Holder, Julian and McKellar, Elizabeth eds., *Neo-Georgian Architecture 1880–1970: a reappraisal* (Historic England, 2016)

McKean, Charles, *The Scottish Thirties: An Architectural Introduction* (Rutland Press, 1987)

Meades, Alan, *Arcade Britannia: A Social History of the British Amusement Arcade* (MIT Press, 2022)

Reading, Billy, *Brutalism* (Amberley, 2018)

Simpson, Eric, *Wish You Were Still Here: The Scottish Seaside Holiday* (Amberley, 2013)

Smith, Janet, *Liquid Assets: The Lidos and Open Air Swimming Pools of Britain* (English Heritage, 2005)

Stamp, Gavin, *Interwar: British Architecture 1919–1939* (Profile Books, 2024)

Toulmin, Vanessa, *Blackpool Pleasure Beach* (Blackpool Council, 2011)

Walton, John K, *The British Seaside: Holidays and Resorts in the Twentieth Century* (Manchester University Press, 2000)

Wood, Ghislaine ed., *Art Deco by the Sea* (Sainsbury Centre, Norwich, 2020)

ACKNOWLEDGEMENTS

It takes a lot of people to make a book but the first hurdle to overcome is convincing a publisher that your idea has merit. I am very grateful to the late and much-missed Elain Harwood for her early support and the suggestion that I approach her publisher. Catherine Croft also lent me her backing from the outset, along with that of C20 Society, and I am thrilled that she has contributed the Afterword. It was Catherine who suggested I take a selection of postcards to show Polly Powell and it was those that defined the look and shape of the book. In Polly I found a wonderfully sympathetic publisher and having another seaside enthusiast for an editor has been a delight. It has been a real pleasure working with Nicola Newman.

I also wish to thank my seaside friends and colleagues, especially Anya Chapman, Allan Brodie, Fred Gray, Geoffrey Mead and Andrew Emery. Thanks too, to Tim Gale and Otto Saumarez-Smith for readily sharing their respective research on Rhyl and leisure centres. Neil Thomas-Childs did a fantastic job as my eyes on the ground in Torquay and Paignton, which massively helped my understanding of progress there, and for which I owe him a big thank you. I am also grateful to the staff at Lowestoft Local Studies Library who gave me their time when they were busy with other things, to Vittorio Ricchetti at Southend Museum, Jonny Ellis at Great Yarmouth Library and the Bournemouth Heritage Librarians. For their help with specific queries about Weymouth Pavilion and Skegness Pier I would like to thank Nathan Elphick of Verity and Beverley Architects and John Morgan at Leonard Design Architects. Darren Walker kindly sought out information about Great Yarmouth Tower and Michael Ferry researched the Landmark Theatre at Ilfracombe. Via Twitter (X) I have found an enthusiastic and generous community who have frequently helped answer my questions and shared material they thought might be of use to me. In this context I would particularly like to thank Ron Wessels, Susan Fielding, Alison Tarada, Sandra Ward, Robert Walton, James Bettley and Chrissie Burgess. I must also mention the dealers at the East Grinstead Collectors Fair for providing me with postcards to look through every month.

To my children, Felix, Arthur and Honor, who sometimes wonder why I don't get a 'proper job', I hope they forgive the months of me being distracted and working evenings now they can see the end result. Finally, to my lovely husband Matthew, for being my sounding board, editor and best friend, thank you.

POSTCARD PUBLISHERS

Thanks for help with reproduction rights goes to Ian Wallace, Caroline Jarrold, Lucinda Gosling, Charles Salmon, John Edward Linden, Rosemary Pearson, Neal Elliott, Terry Nigh and Trevor Wolford. The following publishers have been kind enough to grant permission to reproduce their work: Aero Pictorial (Historic England Archive), Bamforth and Co., Elgate Products Limited, Jarrold, John Hinde Archive (Mary Evans Picture Library), The J Salmon Image Archive, Judges of Hastings.

Every effort has been made to trace all original publishers who are listed below. Should any new copyright information be made known to the publishers this will be acknowledged in future editions of the book.

Pages 85, 98: Aero Pictorial © Historic England Archive; 4, 75, 132, 133, 144, 147, 149, 181, 196 Bamforth and Co.; 170 Walter S Bone, Maidstone;173 Percy Butler, Parkstone, Poole (White Heather, Aberdeen);195, 200 Colourmaster, Crawley; 88 D Constance Limited, Littlehampton, Sussex; 60 Dean, Sandown, Isle of Wight; 24, 111, 142, 159, 163, 166, 167, 178, 192, 199, 203, 205, E T W Dennis & Sons Ltd., Scarborough; 208 Dennis / John Hinde; 28 Donlion Productions, Doncaster; 209 J Arthur Dixon / John Hinde; 91, 164, 169, 174, Elgate; 190, 204 Europa Cards, Ashton Reed, Paignton; 69, 70 Excel series; 101 Hamilton-Fisher and Co, Torquay, Devon; 152 J Hammersley, Boscombe; 143 Harvey Barton, Bristol; 93,115, 127, 135, Jarrold & Sons Ltd., Norwich © Jarrold; 30, 45 Judges Limited, Hastings; 213 John Edward Linden; 128 Mason's Alpha Series; 121 W J Nigh & Sons Ltd, Ventnor; 34 NPO Belfast Ltd., Belfast; 191 Palgrave; 66, 95,106, Photochrom, Tunbridge Wells; 136 Photographic Greeting Card Co Ltd., London; 7, 109, 119, 125, 130, 160, 175, 180, 183, 185, 187, 188 Photo Precision Limited/ Colourmaster, St Ives, Huntingdon; 38 © Rosemary Pearson; 124, 184, 206, 210, 214, The J Salmon Image Archive; 116 Sanderson & Dixon, Ambleside; 55, 94, 103 Shoesmith and Etheridge Ltd, Hastings; 56 E A Sweetman, Tunbridge Wells; 139 W S Thomson, Edinburgh; 39, 42 Raphael Tuck & Sons Ltd; 12, 15, 19, 27, 35, 47, 48, 49, 62, 68, 74, 79, 84, 102, 105, 148, 151, 153, 176 Valentine & Sons Ltd, Dundee; 82 Whiteholme (Publishers) Ltd, Dundee; 141 C G Williams, Worthing; 2, 11, 17, 18, 21, 22, 25, 31, 33, 36, 41, 44, 53, 59, 63, 65, 73, 76, 80,81, 87, 90, 96, 99, 112, 117, 122, 129, 138, 154, 157 unknown publishers.

INDEX

ABOUT THE AUTHOR

Kathryn Ferry has been researching and writing about the British seaside since she fell in love with beach huts back in 1998. With a background in architectural history, she worked for the Victorian Society after completing her PhD at the University of Cambridge. She is now an independent historian and lecturer with more than ten books to her name including *Seaside 100: A History of the British Seaside in 100 Objects* and the official history of Butlin's.

Kathryn is a founder member of the Seaside Heritage Network, a former Media Officer for the National Piers Society and a Fellow of the Royal Historical Society. She also regularly shares her love of the seaside on television and radio.

@SeasideFerry
www.kathrynferry.co.uk
www.seasideheritage.org.uk